Lutz Peschke/Can Gürmeriç (eds.)

Online Communication
in the Context of Personal, Virtual and Corporate Identity Formation

Lutz Peschke/Can Gürmeriç (eds.)

Online Communication in the Context of Personal, Virtual and Corporate Identity Formation

Bibliografische Information der Deutschen Nationalbibliothek:
Die Deutsche Nationalbibliothek verzeichnet diese Publikation in der
Deutschen Nationalbibliografie; detaillerte bibliografische Daten sind im
Internet über http://dnb.dnb.de abrufbar.

Cover picture: Marleen C. Schwalm, Bonn/Germany

Oktober 2018

© 2018 Lutz Peschke/Can Gürmeriç
Herstellung und Verlag:
BoD-Books on Demand, Norderstedt

ISBN: 978-3-7528-3593-9

Index

PART I:
ONLINE COMMUNICATION BETWEEN
PERSONAL AND
VIRTUAL IDENTITIES

Online Identity and Online Anonymity

Lutz Peschke[*]

Introduction

The implementation of digital media in our today's communication has a strong impact on the media behaviours in the society. In the last decades, great importance is given to the protection of the personality rights in the context of the new media. Since our communication is a media based communication, its impact on the construction of reality affects the normative value pattern of societies. To understand new media as a central aspect of our mediatised world, it has to be located and analysed both, in the communicative and normative system. If we consider that we are living in a globalized world, the communicative and normative approach need a comparative study. (Peschke/Güneş Peschke 2016). The internet with all its facets of digital components has a big impact on the construction of reality. According to Luhmann, there is a distinction of two realities, a first reality which is physically experienced and second reality which is observed. But with the implementation of mass media there is a doubling of reality which takes place in the observed system of mass media (Luhmann 2000: 4). This thesis can be transferred to the system of new media. The process of observation is not a pure activity in the physical world anymore. New media enables the participation of information from all over the world. Information is accessible in everywhere and at any time. This virtual observation leads

---

[*] Assts. Prof. Dr. Dr. Lutz Peschke, Bilkent University, Department of Communication and Design. Ankara/Turkey

to a paradox of reality which deals with different distinctions (system/environment) and references (self-reference/other-reference) as if they were the same one. With the generation of a virtual reality, it is hardly possible to distinguish, whether the reality is constructed by experiences or observations. In perception of the new media system, the distinction between the world as it is and the world as it is observed becomes blurred (ibid.: 11). This paper wants to shed light on the so-called dark web from the perspective of communication studies. It will contribute to a better understanding of new media communication on the way to establish a legal and ethical framework.

Social Media Communication

The understanding of media usage needs the discussion in the context to the processes of mediation and mediatization. According to Lundby, mediation is understood as regular mediated communication, which becomes its shape through the process of remediation. Remediation describes the phenomenon that digital media remediates constantly its predecessors (TV, radio, print journals etc.). In distinction to the process of mediation, mediatization conceives and describes long term cultural and social changes initiated and effected by mediated communication. This so-called meta-process is more a transformation process than a change. The central point in it is the social and cultural transformation (Lundby 2014). Thimm points to the characteristics of the ubiquity of media combined with simultaneity, special omnipresence, dislocality and multi-mediality. The usage of digital media is not an exclusive event anymore, but everyday acting (Thimm 2011). The meta-process of mediatization describes the fact, that media penetrates the everyday life in a way, that the usage of media constitutes a big self-evidence even for little children.

These meta-processes of mediatization has a deep impact on the understanding and perception of public and privacy. The term "privacy" is basically defined as a confined space belonging to an individual which is only accessible for a self-determined group of people. The accessibility of the private space is either one of the most critical and most important characteristics of privacy. On the one hand, "privacy" only exists in the distinction of "public". Outside of this private domain there is the public space, where members of that space have to obey rules and where the others have the right to interact with every private person without asking for permission (Güneş Peschke/Peschke 2013; Güneş Peschke 2014: 71). The right to define the private and the public space belongs to the individual. On the other hand, for the formation of the own Self there is a need of permeability between "privacy" and "public". But a survey with academic people in Turkey revealed that with help of social media and influenced by the communication the border between public and privacy is burred (Peschke, 2016).

The study reveals that there are two different groups in their assessment of using Facebook. One group distinguishes between private and public in a traditional way. Entertaining activities like shopping, being engaged with hobbies and spending time with friends are exclusively localized in the public space. The private space is divided into the private privacy, where the intimate activities like praying, spending time with the family, writing a love letter as well as social activities are located, and the personal privacy, where reading newspapers, going to the polls and the career (working, giving a presentation) are situated. Using Facebook is located in the public space, but at the border to the private space. In the life world of the first experimentee group, there is a sharp border between public and private media activities. The exchange of personal data occurs only in an inner circle of family members and close friends. The meaning of the decision what to reveal and what to conceal of own personal data is clearly identifiable. Revealing of own personal data is a matter of the public sphere. In a second experimentee group a bigger permeability of privacy and public can be identified. On one side entertainment is not only limited to the public sphere. Hobbies, activities with friends as well as shopping and social activities are regarded as private activities. Thus, the private sphere can be divided into the private privacy (family life, praying, writing a love letter and working) and public privacy with the activities mentioned above. The public sphere can be classified into a serious public with the political activities, going to the polls and reading newspapers and a free time public, where watching TV, giving a presentation, Twitter and Facebook activities are located. The area of entertainment extends to the sphere of public privacy and free time public. The experimentees of the second group locates Facebook activities in the environment of the free time public but understand it as private activities. This shows that between certain private and public domains there exists a broad area with activities which are not classified as private or public by the users in a clear and definite way. This is an indication for a blurring of privacy.

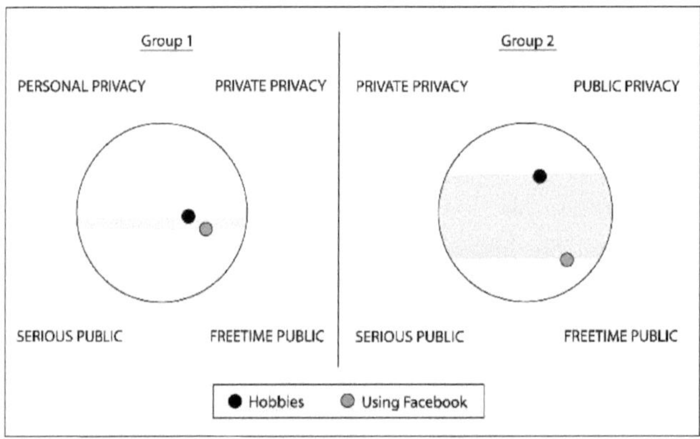

Figure 1: The blurring of public and privacy. (Peschke 2016)

Inside of the discourse about privacy and public it has to be understood that at latest since the beginning of the digital age, the balance between forgetting and remembering is changed. Before the penetration of digital media into everyday life, forgetting was the norm and remembering was the exception. The very most activities were influenced by the desire not to be forgotten. Many books are written, museums, libraries and their archives are established just to save knowledge about the cultural heritages. Today, in the digital age nearly everybody generates digital traces in the internet cloud which can be easily identified and found with help of the powerful search engines. The phenomenon that the web hardly forgets is, that people do not have to give too much to be remembered but it is very difficult and nearly impossible to erase all personal traces from the web. As consequence, remembering became the norm and forgetting is an exception (Meyer-Schönfelder 2009). The consequence is an increasing risk of the infringement of the personality rights. The mediatized world generated a right to be forgotten which is hardly to defend (Peschke 2015).

Surveillance

But our media based communication is not only limited on communication between human beings. Rather, the human machine interaction is highly influences by the internet of things. An increasing number of households are IP controlled. Coffee machines, heaters, light and lockers etc. can be navigated from outside. We are able to control our home from everywhere we are with help of a smart home concept. Additionally, via GPS we are able to navigate our cars easily to a defined place, even if we have never been there before. But every signal what we can use to find information can identify and find our location and preferences as well. Every WLAN spot what we like to use with our mobile devices locates as much better the GPS signals. The journalist and technology researcher Julia Angwin regards the smartphone as a spy master's dream. The former Central Intelligence Agency (CIA) employee Edward Snowden concludes that the "web we loved been turned against us". As a consequence, there is a big need to rethink the web philosophy and concepts, because user's data are not analysed by people but by computer programmes, as the inventor of the internet Tim Berners Lee mentioned (BBC 2014). Machines learn how to observe data and how to spot trends. At least, when Snowden leaked classified information from the National Security Agency (NSA) greater interest than ever has been generated in how the interest is being used for the purposes of surveillance.

These realizations can be regarded as a turning point in the concept of social media. Until these revelations, social media were in all cases understood as a user generated content platform which created a powerful bottom-up tool with a big impact of democratization of content and opinion generation as well as the risks and significant legal consequences in this context. But latest the revelations of Edward Snowdon and Chelsea Manning in combination with the establishment of WikiLeak by Julian Assange demonstrated that there are a huge number of surveillance programs which use the internet and especially the user generated data for their own interest. Many of them run by intelligence services, especially by NSA. It is enabled by the fact that collecting and watching data is no longer a business of human power. Rather machines learnt how to observe data and how to spot trends with it. Today, it can be understood, that collecting and watching data are not only done by governmental organizations, but also by a large number of business people. With help of digital algorithms, they are able to understand all online movements and digital habits of users in order to make their business and marketing strategies more effective and powerful. It is understood that in our mediatised world the internet habits of the society are the window to the most detailed and private information of the user. These data are collected with the aim to sell them for highest prizes to interested companies. It means that collecting data become an extremely lucrative branch in the economy. These developments signify the turning point in social media. They are not a bottom-up platform anymore which gives the power to the user and strengthens democratic movements. It is completely under control by professionals, business makers and hegemonic interest groups with surveillance purposes. Because of the big number of data, it is easily possible to identify every kind of personal information (Peschke 2017). With help of the so-called factor analysis the very most human traits can be reduced to five dimensions of personality, independent of language and culture. These are the so-called Big Five, which includes openness, consciousness, extroversion, agreeableness, and neuroticism. Openness considers cultural and intellectual aspect. It evaluates criteria like appreciation for art, emotional behaviours, unusual ideas, curiosity and different aspects of experiences. Consciousness takes into consideration the degree of self-discipline, how dutiful the user acts and if he/she plans his/her life or if he/she is more a spontaneous type. Extroversion considers energetic parameters, positive emotions, and the tendency of a person to seek stimulation and the company of others. Agreeableness evaluates the tendency to be compassionate and cooperative rather than suspicious and antagonistic towards others. As the fifth dimension, neuroticism checks the tendency how a person deals with unpleasant emotions, such as anger, anxiety, depression, or vulnerability (oaks.nvg.org). These are subsumed under the acronym OCEAN. With help of the OCEAN profile all people can be understood according to their habits and opinions. According to Grassegger and Krogerus the psychologist Konsinski had developed a method, how human can be analysed according to their facebook activities at any time. It is said, that this method supported Donald Trump to win the presidential elections in 2016 (Grassegger/Krogerus 2016). Intelligent environments as described above are increasingly pervasive, because they are implemented in wide range of contexts. As consequence, they raise many ethical and social issues. Jones et al. outlined and classified the upcoming and already existing activities as a contribution for an ethical framework for intelligent environments' development (Jones et al. 2015).

Way into an Online Anonymity?

Considering these facts, the central questions arise, how to protect mass on surveillance. In order to have a free society, users have to have freedom of analysis about behavior and about communication. According to cryptographer David Chaum, these fundamental rights can only be protected, if the users will be turned into anonymous user. The US government understood the importance of protecting their own communication and started a research programme. US Naval Research Center created the TOR network (TOR = The Onion Router) with a special way of encryption. This enabled that the user is hidden with the result, that anonymous surfing in the internet is possible (BBC, 2014). The internet community celebrated quite rightly the TOR concept as the solution for the protection of privacy, freedom of speech with a high potential of democratising effect. But the TOR network did not only protect users with a good and purposes. It also provides a platform for illegal activities and business, the so-called DarkNet. One prominent example of the DarkNet was Silk Road which was as a global drugs market place which brought together anonymous buyers and sellers from all around the world. Silk Road attracted new customers for illegal deals. They could manage their business offsidely from any control and regulations. Their advantage was, that the dark website is impossible to shut down because nobody knows where the dark websites are hosted. Business in the dark web is supported by the new currency Bitcoin. Bitcoins do exist only online. The virtual money can be moved anonymously without any bank involvement. As a consequence, bank and government cannot control it but it is only controlled by an algorithm since it is an electronic cash, handled by a cryptographic key. These hidden and illegal businesses lead to the question, whether anonymity is predominantly a threat to the society. Does anonymity offered by TOR network encourage crime or does it simply displace it? According to Eugene Kaspersky's opinion "critical services like finance services need an online passport. There is a balance between freedom and security, anonymity and showing your ID. […] If you want to travel, if you want to pay with credit card, if you want to access internet, forget about privacy" (BBC 2014). His opinion about the loss of privacy during public activities can be a suitable seed crystal for an important urgently needed discourse which includes all legal and ethical aspects.

Conclusion

In this paper certain the turn of social media from a democratic and user generated content platform to a market place of Big Data were described and discussed. Within the scope of this turn is the question why the internet industry promise decentralization but moves to centralization and control where only a few global players (Google, Facebook, Apple, Amazon) rules the online world. According to Lovink (2016: 29) this question is not understood and remains unanswered for now. To avoid surveillance and control as well as getting reduced on being a profitable set of data anonymity has become increasingly associated with the maintenance of a free society. But in the other side, the shadow of anonymity generates space for trolling, cyberbullying and illegal business. The revelation of that activities needs the potential identifiability of individuals and has to be discussed in legal, ethical and communicational context.

References

BBC (2014): Horizon. Inside of the dark web. Retrieved from https://topdocumentaryfilms.com/inside-dark-web/ [Last access: 07.10.2017]

Grassegger, Hannes / Krogerus, Mikael (2016): Ich habe nur gezeigt, dass es die Bombe gibt. Das Magazin. Retrieved from https://www.dasmagazin.ch/2016/12/03/ich-habe-nur-gezeigt-dass-es-die-bombe-gibt/ (last access: 12.05.2017)

Güneş Peschke, Seldağ (2014). Roma Hukukundan Günümüze Kişilik Haklarının Korunması. Ankara: Yetkin.

Güneş Peschke, Seldağ / Peschke, Lutz (2013): Protection of the Mediatized Privacy in the Social Media: Aspects of the Legal Situation in Turkey and Germany. Gazi University Faculty of Law Review, 17 (1-2): 857-883.

Jones, Simon / Hara, Sukhvinder; Augusto, Juan Carlos (2015): eFriend: an ethical framework for intelligent environments development. Ethics and Information Technology, 17(1), 11-25.

Lovink, Geert (2016): Social media abyss : critical internet cultures and the force of negation. Cambridge/UK: Polity

Luhmann, Niklas (2000): Reality of Mass Media. Standford: Stanford University Press.

Lundby, Knut (2014): Mediatization of Communication. Berlin/Boston: De Gruyter.

Mayer-Schönberger, Viktor (2009): Delete. The Virtue of Forgetting in the Digital Age. Princeton University Press.

Peschke, Lutz (2017): New Media Between User Generated Content and Professionalism. Saarbrücken/Balti: Lambert Academic Press.

Peschke, Lutz (2016): The Relevance Patterns of Public and Privacy for Digital Natives in Turkey. TRT akademi 'Digital Media', vol 01 (02) July 2016, pp. 366-386.

Peschke, Lutz (2015): "The Web Never Forgets": Aspects of the Right to Be Forgotten. Gazi University Faculty of Law Review, 19 (1): 117-126.

Peschke, Lutz; Güneş Peschke, Seldağ (2016): New Media Between Communicative and Normative Studies. In: Güneş Peschke, Seldağ / Peschke, Lutz (eds.): New Media and Law. A Comparative Study. Ankara: Yetkin.

Thimm, Caja (2011): Ökosystem Internet – Zur Theorie digitaler Sozialität. In: Anastasiadis, Mario; Thimm, Caja (eds.): Social Media. Theorie und Praxis digitaler Sozialität. Frankfurt a.M./New York: Peter Lang.

Creating Ideal Selfs.
Self-Presentation Strategies by Using Online Dating Platforms

Kardem Dim[*]

Abstract

The question of the research paper is how the users present their "ideal self" online in digital dating platforms by using "self-presentation strategies", comparing and contrasting online relationships to face-to-face relationships, regarding the users' behaviors both online and in real world. In this paper, social determinism and technological determinism will be defined and analyzed through the context of "digital dating" and Goffman's work of "self- presentation" will be used in order to reveal how the users present themselves online when it comes to initiate romantic relationships. As a mainstream social practice, dating online is a new habit of most of the people in the world, who experience the process of relationship formation and dissolution, the nature of self-disclosure, methods of conflict management and the meaning of infidelity in online platforms. On this account, during the process of the research, "qualitative data" will be used by conducting interviews with the people between 18-27 ages of young adults who live in Ankara, Turkey. Especially the people who use Tinder will share their experiences of "self- presentation" and online romantic relationships. Besides, their experiences will be indicating how a country's cultural aspects influence the perspective of online dating, as well as influencing the usage of dating

[*] Kardem Dim, Bilkent University, Department of Communication and Design. Ankara/Turkey

websites in a country. Gender differences in digital dating will also be discussed in a small part of the paper. Throughout the research paper, key words such as "intimacy", "anonymity", "honesty", "change of cultural norms", "computer-mediated communication and relationship", "pressures" and "desires" will be defined and discussed as the terms which are related to the subject. Consequently, a brief description of what digital dating is will be given in the paper, later "the users" in online dating platforms will be focused by covering the topics which were mentioned above. The aim of the paper is to display how the users' behaviors are shaped in digital dating platforms.

Introduction

From the beginning of humanity, humans seek love and sense of belonging. In every era, the way that humans seek love and sense of belonging had changed and it has been changing or transforming, even today. With the existence of printed advertisements in 1960s and 1970s, people began to search for potential partners. By giving their personal advertisements which include a description of the person's qualities, type of the desired relationship and the qualities of potential partner, people used to seek relationship. However, these types of advertisements were not frequently used (Finkel et al. 2012). In 1980s, video-dating was emerged which included profile descriptions, photographs and a brief videotaped interview. There was an initial screening based on the user's photos and profile information. Later, the people used to view the users' videotapes which interested them most. After they used to express interest for the potential partners and if the interest was mutual, they used to exchange their contact information, so couples could meet face-to-face (ibid.). "Just as printed personal advertisements followed the emergence of newspapers, and just as video-dating followed the emergence of video cassette recorders, computer-based matching services followed the emergence of computers" (ibid., 7). In the course of time, online dating became a widespread phenomenon which most of the people began to see it as a significant tool to find potential mates.

"Interactants in online environments experience same pressures and desires, but the greater control over self-presentational behavior in CMC allows individuals to manage their online interactions more strategically" (Ellison et al. 2006). Due to online platforms enable users to introduce themselves in different ways, the possibility of having an honest relationship is questioned. Besides, internet provides more freedom than real life environment which can be harmful for the people. The main reason of this situation is some people may have romantic or sexual desires which are not acceptable for the community they live in. Due to these desires cannot be expressed in real life; these desires are not fulfilled and usually suppressed as abnormal feelings. Moreover, most of the people tend to tell lies in order to be liked or loved by another person.

Human relationships are complicated due to there are lots of factors which influence a relationship. Physical appearance is one of the most significant factors, because "chemistry" is essential initiate or even to maintain a relationship. Other than chemistry, being compatible is important. Especially having common values, desires and similar characters are strong factors for the relationship. On the other hand, these values and desires are mostly determined by social environments.

Dating styles ranges throughout generations. Besides, expected relationship with opposite sex determines new criteria for potential mates. For example, in a short time sexual relationship, potential mates' physical appearance and availability for sex based relationships may be the most significant criteria, rather than having compatible character qualities and housework skills. At the same time, polygamy is frequently pursued in online dating and infidelity highly occurs in online dating platforms. It can be said that "morality" which is determined by society's and religion's rules does not exist in online dating platforms.

Fidelity is essential for almost every relationship. However, the definition of fidelity may be different, when it comes to online dating. Due to couples may communicate from different cities and even from different countries; it may not be a problem to satisfy their sexual needs with another person which is closer to themselves in terms of space.

Although the possibility of having a healthy relationship via online dating platforms is dubious, it seems like an effective solution for the people who want to meet more people by not being limited by their social circles and its psychological and moral pressures.

Theories

Romantic relationships have always been one of the most significant areas of human life. Since the beginning of the world, humans aim to find their partners in order to supply emotional and sexual needs. Before the invention of Internet, people used to supply these needs in different ways. They had limited options in the society they live in and they were usually looking for someone, a third person from their family or society, to find a potential mate. With the rise of technology, Internet became a new tool for searching a potential partner and people began to use online dating sites. In this paper, online dating will be analyzed in terms of Goffman's work of "self-presentation" (1959), Maslow's Hierarchy Pyramid (1987) social determinism and technological determinism will be discussed and analyzed as the basic theories of online dating. (Hogan 2010) Throughout the research paper, key words such as "intimacy", "anonymity", "honesty", "change of cultural norms", "computer-mediated communication and relationship", "pressures" and "desires" will be defined and discussed as the terms which are related to the subject. The aim of the paper is to display how the users' behaviors in online dating platforms will be focused by covering the topics which were mentioned above.

Goffman's dramaturgical approach which includes the notions of front and back stage focuses on situations (Hogan 2010). According to Goffman, people usually act in a different way in order to impress other people in the society and they display themselves in an active way to earn an effective place in other people's minds. Interaction with the other people indicates the "front stage". On the other hand, a person also has a "back stage" which is the time when he is alone in his private space. When it comes to online dating, people tend to display themselves in a different way in order to impress a possible romantic partner. Due to satisfy the need of being accepted and loved (which is explained in Maslow's Hierarchy Pyramid), the online dating users tend to deceive other online dating users which give harm to "honesty". Even though this type of behavior is unethical, it has a strong reason to act like that. "The need to connect deeply with others has been described as a fundamental human motivation." (Baumeister / Leary 1995). This need makes online dating users to lie and deceive other users. Stereotypes and prejudgments are frequently existed not only in real life, but also in online dating sites. Especially the users tend to lie about their physical appearances due to physical attraction (chemistry) is a significant factor to initiate a relationship. According to a survey conducted on over 4000 online daters, the users choose to date with another user which has the same racial background with them and most of the users avoid dating with black people, as a result of racial prejudgment. Besides, users want to date with a user who shares similar background and characteristics or hobbies with them. This tendency of choosing an online dating partner according to these qualities has a reason which is "sharing a higher compatibility". (Kee / Yazdanifard 2015) The algorithms of dating sites are designed to "match" the users by looking at their profile similarities. That is to say, Goffman's front and back stage is highly related with the subject of online dating and using online dating strategies seems as an accurate consequence to impress potential romantic partners. However, most of the time the users face to heartbreaks and disappointments when they meet their online dating partners in real life, in a face-to-face conversation. When the users' expectations of their ideal partners do not fit the reality of a potential partner, it turns into a combination of heartbreak and disappointment.

The preference of using online dating sites highly in today's era is based on some sources which are to search for new friends and new sex partners, ease boredom, relaxation, finding romantic partners and having more options at once while satisfying these needs (ibid.). Although there are lots of disadvantages of online dating and it causes some unethical behaviors like deceiving and cheating other users, people prefer to use online dating sites such as Tinder and OK Cupid to experiment online dating. Today, internet matchmaking became a common perception that online dating is a viable, efficient way to meet dating or long-term relationship partners. (St. John 2002) Two different perspectives can be used to today's online dating platforms which are the theories of "Technologically deterministic perspective" and "Socially deterministic approach". While "Technologically deterministic perspective" focuses on the characteristics of the technologies themselves, "Socially deterministic approach" privileges user behavior and social shaping of technology approaches. Though both of the approaches are beneficial to analyze today's digital dating phenomenon, "Technologically deterministic perspective" seems to provide a more reliable approach. Due to technological determinism focuses on technology's effect on society structure, it can be said that today's high Internet usage and existence of online dating platforms caused people's behaviors to communicate and choose their partners online. Besides, the tendency to lie on online dating platforms, to search for polygamy and infidelity became widespread with the opportunity to reach and satisfy all needs online. Sex, pornography, erotic chat rooms create another dimension of computer mediated relationships which indicate that sexual desires can be fulfilled via Internet. "Online dating sites give people the idea of bigger social circle and larger number of potential mates." (Kee / Yazdanifard 2015) Because of this, people prefer to meet online with their potential partners rather than meeting them in a traditional way, which is "face-to-face" relationship.

Computer mediated and face-to-face relationships have some similarities and distinctions between them. In face-to-face romantic relationships, the most significant factors for a relationship are spatial proximity, physical attractiveness, discovery of similarities and self-disclosure. For the individuals in computer mediated relationship there is no importance for spatial proximity due to it enables to communicate everyone all over the world more quickly and intimately. Thus, computer mediated relationship makes interacting to another person easy and it causes less pressures from family and friends, due to the online romantic partner does not involve in the same social circle that the other user does. Besides, computer mediated relationships enable a psychological comfort. The reason of this psychological comfort is based on being unknown by the other user and the information which is given in online dating platforms are limited. The personal information in online dating platforms is dependent on the users' will and control. Unlike face-to-face relationships, having a psychological comfort in computer mediated relationship enables easy to break-up by avoiding, ignoring and controlling situations that cause discomfort or annoyance. In computer mediated relationship, users can choose not answering electronic messages or logging off the computer which enables to avoid any kinds of conflict management. That is to say, both maintaining and ending a face-to-face relationship is more difficult when it is compared to computer mediated relationships. These features of online dating motivate people to be brave while initiating and ending a relationship.

Moreover, the meaning of infidelity changes in computer mediated relationships due to geographical separation of partners. There are different types of infidelity which are emotional, sexual and emotional-sexual infidelity. Although infidelity is a major problem for traditional relationships, in computer mediated relationships it seems more flexible due to less or without physical contact between the partners. Even though traditional face-to-face relationships are harder to maintain and end, these types of relationships usually provide more "honesty" and "reliability" when it is compared to online relationships. Since trust is one of the most important elements of every relationship, face-to-face relationship seems to satisfy this need.

Gender difference is another issue of online dating. Men and women tend to act in a different way while dating online. "Females have been found to generally self-disclose more about their fears and weaknesses than males." (Jourard 1971) Furthermore, online dating enables both genders to communicate equally and comfortably, because there is no pressure from society, especially for females. Low pressure from society seems like an advantage for the online dating site users. However, low pressure also enables unethical behaviors online which can lead to harmful consequences such as spreading sexual transmitted diseases.

In conclusion, the users' attitudes in online dating platforms will be analyzed according to the theories of Goffman's dramaturgical approach (back stage, front stage), Maslow's Hierarchy Pyramid, social determinism, technological determinism. Besides, the similarities and differences between computer mediated relationship and face-to-face relationship will be explained by giving examples. By considering terms of "intimacy", "anonymity", "honesty", "change of cultural norms", "pressures" and "desires", the effect of online dating platforms to today's relationship formations will be questioned and discussed throughout the paper. Qualitative data will also be used by conducting an interview about Tinder with ten people among Bilkent University students. In this interview, the questions which are related to the social and psychological theories will be answered.

Research

The question of the research paper is how the users present their "ideal self" online in digital dating platforms by using "self-presentation strategies", comparing and contrasting online relationships to face-to-face relationships, regarding the users' behaviors both online and in real world. In order to display how the users' behaviors are shaped in digital dating platforms, a research is carried out.

Throughout the research, interviews were made with the university students between 18 – 27 ages who live in Ankara, Turkey. Ten participants are attended to the interview. Five of them are female and five of them are male. The number of the participants is designed to include equal number of females and males, so the gender differences can be clearly observed throughout the research. Most of the interviews are conducted face-to-face and other interviews are conducted on telephone or via e-mail. Qualitative data is used in the research; however, while putting the answers into the categories, quantitative data is also used. The survey's questions are about Tinder usage and young adults answered these questions by adding their own perceptions about online dating. That is to say, the strongest point of the data is the variety of answers from different point of views and the weakest point of the data is the complexity of the answers, while gathering them into categories in order to transform them into quantitative data. Due to the dynamics of social relationships are highly flexible and changeable, there are always question marks about the certainty and accuracy of a particular behavior.

The survey is composed of 19/20 answers. The reason that some people are asked one more question is their sexual preferences, because three of the participants are LGBT individuals. These people are asked about the behaviors of LGBT people on Tinder dating platform to analyze the differences when it is compared to heterosexual people's behaviors on online dating platforms. Here are the survey questions which are answered by the university students:

1)   How did you learn that there is an online dating platform like Tinder?

2)   Why did you decide to use Tinder? Why did you feel the need of using Tinder?

3)   Did you find what you were looking for or what you expected on Tinder?

4)   According to you, why do people use Tinder?

5)   Is Tinder used the most among all online dating platforms?

6)   Do people satisfy themselves by using Tinder for fun and new experiences?

7)   Do the people tell lies to each other in order to be liked by the opposite sex (potential love partners)?

8)   Do the people tell lies about their hobbies and biographies or do they tell lies about their physical appearances such as their heights, weights and their ages?

9)   Do the people deceive each other visually by using Photoshop, filters, etc.?

10)   Did you tell any lies about your physical appearance or another special feature about yourself on Tinder?

11)   Do you still use Tinder? If you don't, why did you close it?

12)   Do you use online dating/flirting strategies? If you do, what are the strategies you use on Tinder?

13)   How it feels to meet someone face-to-face for the first time? Is there a difference between meeting someone after you talked him/her on Tinder and meeting someone at first in real life?

14)   Did you meet someone on Tinder and have a long-term romantic relationship?

15)   What differentiates Tinder relationship from a normal face-to-face relationship?

16)   Is there a difference between your aim/expectation from the period that you first began to use Tinder and now?

17)   Why do you prefer meeting other people (opposite sex) on Tinder instead of meeting them in real environment?

18)   Do the people around you who use Tinder are happy?

19)   Do the people who use Tinder only for sexual aims are more satisfied than the others?

20)   Do heterosexual and LGBT individuals use online dating platforms such as Tinder in a different way? If so, what are the differences?

First of all, every participant stated that they didn't tell lies on Tinder about themselves to attract potential love or sex partners. In spite of this, every participant stated that most of the people tell lies about themselves on online dating platforms like Tinder, in order to attract more people. Besides, seven participants told that most of the Tinder users lie about their hobbies and biographies, rather than telling lies about their physical appearances. Their belief is it is hard to continue telling lies about physical appearance, because when couples meet on Tinder, they later want to meet face-to-face and the real appearance of people are revealed in these meetings. Alternatively, participants think that putting beautiful photos with filter and different angles do not count as a lie, because everyone wants to present themselves in a charming way and it is regarded as normal to pick the most beautiful photos of themselves, even though the photos are filtered or designed by Photoshop. Everyone knows that Tinder is based on an algorithm which matches people who like each other's profile photos, so physical appearance is very significant at first place to initiate communication between potential partners. Conversely, everyone knows that hobbies and common personalities are also significant to maintain a relationship and even it may have an effect to initiate a relationship. Thus, most of the Tinder users prefer to lie about their hobbies. One male participant said that his Tinder girlfriend whom he dated for four months told him lies about her hobbies, especially about her musical taste. The participant said that he later found out her lie about her musical taste and it had an effect for him to break-up with his girlfriend. He said that he values the similarity of hobbies and musical taste a lot and he felt deceived because of this situation.

The participants tend to classify the relationships in two branches as sexual relationships and romantic relationships. At the same time, except one participant, every participant told that they learned this platform from their friends and they began to use Tinder by looking at their friends. According to the survey, Tinder is the most widespread online dating platform among all other dating platforms. Most of the participants couldn't give a name of an alternative dating site due to they do not know any other online dating site. Only two of the participants said that there is another popular online dating platform which is called OKCupid. As far as they said, OKCupid is very common among

European users. Five participants stated that they still use Tinder, while other participants said that they closed their Tinder accounts. The reason of closing Tinder accounts is the dissatisfaction of Tinder based relationships. These people, who are dissatisfied, explained that they actually look for sincere romantic relationships which can be long-term relationships. However, they understood that Tinder is not a platform to find sincere and trustworthy relationships. Although they used Tinder for short-term purposes like having sex or fun, they decided not to continue to use Tinder anymore.

When it comes to gender differences on Tinder, the results are the opposite that it was expected. It is seen as a myth that in relationships men pursue for sex and women pursue for romance/love. However, during the interview, except two male participants, most of the males stated that they pursue love in their relationships, rather than having sex. On the other hand, except one female (who is a LBGT individual), other female participants told that they pursue for sex and polygamy in Tinder relationships. At the end of the interview, I told some of the participants that males want love in general and females want sex in general, every participant in both sexes said that they are surprised by the result; even they hardly believe that the answers are true, especially about males. Throughout the research, it is seen that male participants accept the fact they experienced sexual relationships which most of them are short-term. On the other hand, they explain that having "empty sex" is not their ultimate aim in relationships with the opposite sex and they aim to find a steady relationship which is both romantic and sexual.

Asking the three LGBT participants about different dating behaviors between homosexual and heterosexual users on Tinder, they told that homosexuals tend to seek sexual relationships in real life but on online dating sites, homosexuals tend to seek romantic relationships. The LGBT participants believe that in real life heterosexuals tend to seek romantic relationships but on Tinder and online dating sites they seek only for sexual relationships. It is one of the most interesting results of the research.

Every participant expressed that there are some people who seek sex and some people seek romance. They said that the people who expect to have sex partners on Tinder always satisfy their needs, however the people who search love on Tinder usually feel disappointment. The participants also explained the reason why people prefer to use Tinder rather than meeting someone new in real life. People open Tinder accounts because they wonder about online dating, they want to have fun and they want to overcome from their loneliness by finding partners online. During the research, one male participant told that he began to use Tinder because he wondered how to date online. Another male participant told that he opened an account on Tinder because he thought it would be fun and he didn't take it seriously. Other participants (eight people) told that they began to use Tinder because they felt lonely and they thought it would be a solution to use Tinder in order to find partners which will help them to overcome from their loneliness. Correspondingly, every participant stated that Tinder is a platform which cannot provide a serious or a long-term romantic relationship due to most of the Tinder users' aim is to find new sex partners and these are the people who are not able to communicate with other people in real life. In spite of this, participants underline the advantages of Tinder such as Tinder is convenient and practical for people who want to find partners with less effort compared to real life and Tinder provides a large amount of new potential partners unlike real social environments' limited group of people. Besides, Tinder is a comfortable platform to find partners without fear of rejection due to it matches people who like each other. When two people meet online, they feel self-confidence because they already know that they like each other's' physical appearance. However, in the physical life, it is not possible to understand a potential partner's feelings or he/she is attracted immediately which takes time. 100% of the participants told that they have fear of rejection by potential love partners in real life that they may not handle it without being embarrassed.

Consequently, the results of the research indicate that there are some parts which every participant agree with, although there are some aspects that their answers should be separated from each other. The research displays that the users do not use certain tactics or lies in order to present their selves to potential love partners on Tinder, but they accept that there is some kind of staging and presenting to other people to be able to attract them. In addition, all the participants think that almost everyone on Tinder lie about themselves, especially when it comes to their hobbies. It can be said that Goffman's dramaturgical approach is accepted by everyone that people get easily suspicious of each other in online dating platforms. Another significant element about the research is that nobody told they use tactics while communicating with their potential partners on Tinder due to everyone's needs/aims are clear enough to be there as online dating members.

Conclusion

Throughout the paper, online dating is analyzed with specific theories and keywords. The main topics of the paper are self-presentation, satisfying basic needs via online dating, psychological aspects of online dating (difference between computer mediated relationship and face-to-face relationship) and gender differences between the users. These main topics are the factors which shape the users' behaviors in online dating platforms.

The paper initiates a qualitative research which is based on questions and answers, related to the topics. This research enabled to understand the motivation of the users while using Tinder and similar online dating platforms. According to the answers of the users who are young adults between 18-27 ages and who live in Ankara, Turkey, the psychological motivation of using online dating platforms can be very different. Although there are a lot of similarities between the users, it is seen that every individual pursues another goal while using Tinder. While some of the users perceive Tinder as a beneficial platform to find potential love or sex partners, some of the users only use Tinder for fun and new experiences to overcome from their boredom. At the same time, their way of communicating with other people is also significant. According to the survey, every user communicates with their potential partners in a direct way, revealing their basic needs. The reason of being direct is the psychological safety of computer mediated relationship. Unlike face-to-face relationship, computer mediated relationship enables psychological comfort in a situation when a person is rejected. Computer mediated relationship provides the users to hide their emotional vulnerability when they are rejected. Besides, in the first step of dating, Tinder matches people who like each other physically. So, it has an effect of self-confidence in first time, while initiating a conversation with the potential partner.

Another advantage of Tinder which is explained by every participant is the ability to find as many people as possible in a wider social circle without being tired and without waiting. Tinder is found practical by the users to meet new people in a short time and it seems as a great advantage for today's young adults who do not want to wait for someone in a long period of time. They prefer to experience fast relationships and the relationships are easily consumed that every Tinder user pursues polygamy in online dating platforms, although they pursued polygamy for a period of time. These situations can be explained that people are not willing to take emotional responsibility in a relationship and they do not prefer to be stressed and concerned, while maintaining a relationship.

The gap of the qualitative research is the feature that there are variety of perspectives and answers, when it comes to relationships. Due to every person and every relationship has its own characteristics and values, it is hard to generalize every online dating user's dating habits and motivation. Moreover, every research presents different data about self-presentation in online dating. For example, in most of the scholars' sources, people use tactics for self-presentation in online dating. On the other hand, throughout the survey most of the participants explained that they did not use any kind of strategies to impress a potential partner.

However, every participant stated that most of the people tell lies about themselves in terms of self-presentation.

In conclusion, online dating is a social subject which newly entered most of the people's lives. Thus, it is a communication platform which has been developing its own norms and rules. There are a lot of stories to be experienced in that particular subject and it is a new way of communication for romance and sex.

Acknowledgement

This paper was written within the scope of the undergraduate course "Advanced Issues in Communication Studies" (Fall 2017-2018) of the Department of Communication and Design at Bilkent University which was directed by Dr. Dr. Lutz Peschke.

References

Ellison, Nicole / Heino, Rebecca / Gibbs, Jennifer (2006): Managing impressions online: Self-presentation processes in the online dating environment. *Journal of computer-mediated communication*, 11(2), 415-441. Retrieved from https://academic.oup.com/jcmc/article/11/2/415/4617726 Accessed on Apr. 10, 2018.

Finkel, Eli J./Eastwick, Paul W./Karney, Benjamin R. / Reis, Harry T./Sprecher, Susan (2012): Online dating: A critical analysis from the perspective of psychological science. *Psychological Science in the Public Interest*, 13(1), 3-66. Retrieved from http://journals.sagepub.com/doi/abs/10.1177/1529100612436522 Accessed on Apr. 10, 2018.

Hogan, Bernie. (2010): The Presentation of Self in the Age of Social Media: Distinguishing Performances and Exhibitions Online. *Bulletin of Science, Technology & Society*, 30(6), 377-386. Retrieved from http://journals.sagepub.com/doi/abs/10.1177/0270467610385893 Accessed on Apr. 10, 2018.

Kee, Angel Wong An / Yazdanifard, Rashad (2015): The Review of the Ugly Truth and Negative Aspects of Online Dating. *Global Journal of Management and Business Research*. Retrieved from
https://www.journalofbusiness.org/index.php/GJMBR/article/view/1700
Accessed on Apr. 10, 2018.

Merkle, Erich R. / Richardson, Rhonda A. (2000): Digital Dating and Virtual Relating: Conceptualizing Computer Mediated Romantic Relationships. *Family Relations*, 49(2), 187-192. Retrieved from
https://onlinelibrary.wiley.com/doi/full/10.1111/j.1741-3729.2000.00187.x
Accessed on Apr. 10, 2018

Internet Mothers
Studies on the Fine Line Between Acceptance and Rejection

Gizem Bahçecioğlu[*]

Abstract

Social media has already become an important part of people's lives. Together with the significance of social media's place, virtual identities come forward. There are some popular virtual identities on Instagram and YouTube in Turkey which are Internet Mothers, fashion-makeup bloggers and women who are sharing food recipes. "Popular" in this case means who has many followers, likes and comments. Those virtual identities are highly accepted, or absolutely rejected by society. The aim of this paper is to examine people's feelings and behaviors towards popular virtual identities mentioned above. With the help of Tajfel's and Turner's social identity theory and Bibb Latane's social impact theory, this paper clarified that the reason behind acceptance and rejection may be the personal similarities between individuals and virtual identities. In order to understand people's feelings and attitudes towards chosen virtual identities, their comments on social media are observed and a qualitative interview is made with 10 participants who are highly engaged with Instagram and YouTube. According to the interview, people's feelings and attitudes are related to their social identities and interests. As

* Gizem Bahçecioğlu, Bilkent University, Department of Communication and Design. Ankara/Turkey

a result of collected data, it appears that people are more likely to follow and accept those popular virtual identities which they have similarities.

Keywords: acceptance, rejection, virtual identities, Internet mothers, fashion and make up bloggers, food recipes, real identity, similarities

Introduction

Social media has already become an important part of people's lives. Almost everybody has at least one social media account such as Instagram, Twitter or Facebook. They appeared as a communication tool for daily life. People prefer using social media for communication rather than face to face communication. It also provides people to another world which is virtual and online. In this virtual world, people have virtual identities and those virtual identities are so credible and reliable now because people engaged too much in social media. The identities which are created on social media accounts not always represent people's identities in physical world, but they are reliable somehow. Many people believe these virtual identities and accept them as a part of their lives without any doubt. They believe what virtual identities' say and behave accordingly. On the other hand, some others hate those virtual identities and reject them strictly. There is a fine line between acceptance and rejection when people's social media activities such as following, liking and commenting considered. People show their feelings and attitudes on social media by their comments written under the posts. In Turkey, mothers who use social media actively, fashion-make up bloggers and women who are sharing food recipes are very popular now on social media. These virtual identities have many followers, in relation to this they have any lovers and haters. Many females follow those virtual identities on Instagram and YouTube, also pay attention to what they share. The products that fashion and make up bloggers share are bought and tried by many females. The food recipes that some women share on

Instagram and YouTube channels are cooked by their many fellows. What is important in this process is the feedback comes from followers. When they try a product or food recipe, they directly give feedback to those virtual identities by commenting or sending messages. This trial of products or recipes are done without any doubt and this demonstrates their followers highly trust those identities. Another group that gained trust from many people are "Internet Mothers". It is one of the popular group which is accepted and followed by many people. Their name "Internet Mothers" come from their social media activities. They engaged too much with social media, because many people trust them and they gain money from social media. Internet Mothers became popular by sharing photos and videos of their cute children. Some people accept this and write positive comments under the photos of Internet Mothers' children, on the other hand some others find it nonsense and think sharing every moment of their children is not appropriate concerning privacy issues. Not only sharing photos or videos on social media, Internet Mothers also participate conferences, seminars and speeches about child development and mother issues. They are invented to conferences and seminars sometimes as a listener, sometimes as a speaker. Some of them take requests for advertisings with their children. When they attend a seminar or conference, many of their followers go to see and listen to them. Moreover, some of their followers invite Internet Mothers to their cities by writing comments or sending messages. They take care of their advices and follow Internet mothers in order to inform about activities and child development. Followers of Internet Mothers ask many questions about child development, they prefer Internet Mothers to consult about child development issues rather than pedagogues or psychologists. Although some people do not follow Internet Mothers on social media and reject, at least they heard about Internet Mothers. While some people highly accept and trust Internet Mothers, some people completely reject them. Their feeling behind rejection is that Internet Mothers ignore privacy. They always share their daily life activities, family and children, in other words, they are living their lives in front of their followers. From one perspective, they ignore privacy because they share every moment and action of their children, also themselves and their families such as husbands. For example, they share many photos and videos from birthday parties of their children. They share the guests, birthday cake, companies of organization, places and presents. There is only black and white for acceptance and rejection on social media. People's feelings and behaviors towards virtual identities can reveal their characteristics and identities. It may be related to people's social identities and groups they belong in their physical worlds. Following sections will examine people's feelings and behaviors towards virtual identities in the context of social identity theory and social impact theory, with the help of social media comments and interviews.

This research aimed at finding people's feelings and approaches towards popular virtual identities in Turkey. It is an undeniable fact that almost everybody engages in social media. Social media became an important part of people's daily lives. They follow some popular virtual identities and reflect their feelings and attitude directly to them. Popular means "who has many followers and likes on social media" in that case. They either trust them, or reject those identities. There is a fine line between love and hate to virtual identities. Some of popular virtual identities on Instagram and YouTube are observed for the research. According to the observations, it appears that some people really trust virtual identities and see them as someone from their social environment. On the other hand, some others reject them completely. To clarify how are the feelings and attitudes of social media users towards virtual identities, the reasons behind those feelings and attitudes needed to be revealed. The sample group for virtual identities are "Internet Mothers on Instagram", "fashion and make up bloggers on Instagram and YouTube" and "women who are sharing food recipes on Instagram and YouTube". In order to clarify feelings and behaviors of people towards those identities, interviews are done with people who are using Instagram and YouTube every day, articles and some other research about virtual identities and social media are checked, Instagram and YouTube comments written to those specific virtual identities are observed and TEDx Talks are watched as a methodology. This paper benefits from the two theories which are "Social Identity Theory" and "Social Impact Theory".

According to social identity theory developed by Tajfel and Turner (Tajfel / Turner 1979), the groups that people belong to has a big impact on pride and self-esteem on their personalities. An individual doesn't have a self-identity but several identities associated with their groups. So, groups give us a sense of identity by belonging a group. The groups that people belong reinforce personal images. On the other hand, the groups that people don't belong to also help to create personal images. By excluding others and differentiate themselves from other groups which is called "out group", people increase their self-image. If a person perceive himself as a part of a particular group, this is an in-group for him. For example, by saying "Turkey is the best country in the world", Turkish person reinforce his self-image by belonging his in-group. People divided the society into "them" and "us". They have a tendency to categorize other individuals to in-groups and out-groups. The theory indicates that in-group differentiate themselves from out-group to enhance their self-image. Hypothesis of the theory states group members of an in-group will seek to find negative aspects of an out group, thus enhance their self-image. While categorizing and stereotyping, people consider the differences and similarities between groups. Members of same group see themselves similar, but see others -which is out group- different. This type of a discrimination may cause to have prejudices against out group. While deciding in-groups and out-groups, there are 3 processes which are social categorization, social identification and social comparison. After those steps, an individual decides his or her groups and create a social identity. As categorizing objects, people also categorize others in order to understand their social environment. Turks, Germans, Muslims, doctors are examples of social categorization. It eases finding in and out groups. Such categorization provides individuals to know which category they belong and understand themselves, then they adopt appropriate behaviors for their groups. A person may belong to various groups like "a Turkish, Muslim doctor". In the second stage which is social identification, people adopt the identity of their categorized group and behave accordingly to group members. For instance, a deputy acts in a way that another deputies act. Social identification enables people to feel themselves valuable and significant, thus their self-confidence and self-esteem increase. The final stage is social comparison. People have a tendency to compare themselves and their groups (in-group) with other groups (out-group). In order to increase and maintain self-esteem and self-confidence, a person see himself and his group members better than the others, so evaluates out group members in a negative way. According to the social identity theory, those stages determine people's identity in social world. Actually, this situation also same with the social media world, which is called "virtual world". In that virtual world, people are searching for people to follow who are similar to themselves and their groups. They feel themselves close to their in-group members and trust them. To exemplify, teachers giving lectures in same school follow each other on Instagram. In order to show positive feelings, they like the posts that their in-group members shared and write positive comments. On the other hand, they tend to reject others which are not close to them, in other words their out-groups. They create a competition between "others" and reject them by not following on social media or writing bad comments. Individuals' social media activities represents their social identities in virtual world. They respond to their in-group members and out-group members by liking their posts, commenting on the posts, following or not following. Those activities in social media world related to their social identities.

Another theory examined in this paper is "Social Impact Theory" developed by Bibb Latané (1981). The theory reveals how people conform to the group they belong, follow and imitate each other. It also indicates the reasons for likelihood that a person will respond to social influence. If a person is under a social force and if he changes his behaviors because of this pressure, it is called "social impact". Social force consists of 3 laws which are strength, immediacy and numbers. Strength is how much power the person influencing someone has (Rowe). For example, if a person has a reputation in society, his orders are more powerful on an individual. Immediacy is how the influence recent and close to the person. For more recent and close order, people are more likely to influenced by the order. If a teenager's father called him and give an order 2 minutes ago, he is more likely to influenced. Numbers are related to the people. The more people putting pressure on an individual to do something, the more social force he has. Conformity is an important concept for individuals' behaviors in society. People's behaviors on social media related to the social influence. If they are under social force, they may feel like they belong to a specific group and try to behave like those group members because of the social force. In some cases, individuals may feel themselves like they have to belong a group in order to have a social identity. To illustrate, if a person's family put pressure on him about political beliefs, he may feel like he has to believe in same way with his family. This situation may impress his activities on social media. He is more likely to follow the leaders of a specific political party which he is under pressure to support and appreciate them by liking and writing comments. Oppositely, he doesn't follow leaders of opposition political parties, he may also write bad and humiliating comments on their posts. To sum up, social force and social influence has an impact on people's behaviors in virtual world, as it has on social identities.

A research found in "Stanford Encyclopedia of Philosophy" written by Shannon Vallor helped forward for this research paper. The research which is called "Social Networking and Ethics" gives information about new media technologies for social networking such as Facebook, Twitter and YouTube. Social networking began to transform the social, political and informational practices of individuals and institutions (Vallor 2016). This research paper utilized from Borgmann's "Critique of Social Hyper-reality". According to Borgmann, there is a hyper-reality which social networking services affect or displace individuals organic and physical identities by allowing people to "offer one another stylized versions of themselves for amorous or convivial entertainment rather than allowing the fullness and complexity of their real identities to be engaged" (Borgmann 1992). Borgman is supporting the idea that social networking services change people's physical identities and create a hyper-reality. The virtual world seems so glamorous that people want to forget hardness's of their lives in this social networking world. This can be a reason for people to accept or reject popular virtual identities. People may see virtual world as an escape from their real and physical lives. They may see those virtual identities as their friends or a part of their lives. Another part which is important in Vallor's paper is "Friendship, Virtue and The Good Life on Social Networking Services". In this part, the author emphasizes that social networking services help people to establish relationships. Because of having more friends or in other words more followers on social media, individuals may think they have many friends and they are popular. This idea of being popular can lead them to follow popular virtual identities -who have many followers and gain many people's trust- on social media.

To conclude, those theories and research paper are beneficial for this paper to understand the feelings and attitudes of people towards virtual popular identities. Being popular for this area means having a lot of followers and gaining many people's trust. Individuals' social activities such as liking, commenting and following reflects their feelings directly. The question needed to be examined is why people accept and trust or reject and don't trust those popular virtual identities.

Description of the Method

This paper utilized from qualitative methods such as qualitative interviews and social media comments. Qualitative methods help understanding problems and ideas by emphasizing meanings, experiences, thoughts and views of the participants. It provides researchers to examine the problem in more detailed way. Economic, political, cultural and environmental factors affect individuals' views and behaviors. For this reason, while making a research on a specific issue, researcher should understand those factors in order to find more reliable results. This type of a method helps researchers to understand participants, context and reactions. It requires specific target group, so it is easier to understand the reactions and behaviors of the participants. For this research, data collected from the interviews with focus group and social media comments of participants. Social media comments written to the sample group are significant for this paper, because those comments directly reflect people's feelings. Comments under the posts of sample group which consist of Internet Mothers, fashion and make-up bloggers and women who are sharing food recipes are observed in order to see how people react to those people. For interviews, qualitative methods are used. The questions asked to the participants are concerning their personal views and experiences. 7 qualitative questions asked to the participants. These are "How do you choose the people you follow on social media?", "Do you know Internet Mothers, do you follow them? Why or why not?", "Do you follow fashion and make up bloggers? Why?", "Do you follow the women who are sharing food recipes? If you follow, do you try their recipes?", "Do you follow any people that you really like?", "Are there any people that you really don't like and don't understand why they are that much popular?", "Do you have similarities with the people you follow and like?". Those are the questions asked to the 10 participants. 6 of the 10 participants are mothers, the rest are university students. Interview questions are determined according to the participants' engagement with the social media. Target group consist of women, because the sample groups are generally interests of target group. Mothers, food recipes, fashion and make up bloggers correlate with females. Their direct responses are focus of this research. Participants' social media activities are observed before the interview questions are prepared. Their Instagram accounts are followed, in addition to this, frequency of their likes and comments are checked every day. After the observation, it arises that all participants are using Instagram and YouTube actively, they highly engaged with social media. All participants are women, their ages are between 20 and 40. The aim of the interview is to find out how the feelings and attitudes of the people towards popular virtual identities are, and the reasons behind them.

Analysis of the Data

According to the results of the interview and the comments written to the posts of specific popular virtual identities people's feelings and attitudes are related to their social identities and interests. The comments written under the posts of sample group demonstrate people have strong feelings to those virtual identities. They either love or hate sample group extremely and show their feelings by writing long comments under the posts. The people who love sampled virtual identities also trust strongly. There is a fine line between acceptance and rejection, feelings of people are extreme. People either love and accept or hate and reject those virtual identities. Moreover, these feelings are at a high level. People from the "love and accept" side appreciate every behavior and speech. They write comments as if they are friends or family. In their comments, they always use lovely words and lovely emoji to show their love. 3 of the most popular Internet mothers are observed for this research. Those mothers have more than hundred thousand of followers. They generally share photos and videos of their children, introduce some products about children and give information about child development. The people who love and accept Internet mothers write lovely comments under the photos of their children and ask questions about child development. They take into consideration the advices of Internet Mothers, moreover, sometimes they send photos to Internet mothers with the products that Internet mothers recommended. Most of them don't even see those Internet mothers, but they love and accept them as they are friends or family. So, they trust people they have never seen before and take advices for their children.

The unusual part of this trust is that none of those Internet Mothers have a university education about child development, so none of them graduated from psychology or child development in their physical lives. One of the Internet Mother introduced herself as a psychologist and pedagogue in a television program, but in her physical life she is not a psychologist or pedagogue. Her followers always ask questions about their children and she respond them as a psychologist and pedagogue. A group of people who mistrust her started investigations against her and they found out that she didn't take education of psychology or pedagogy. She ignored the claims and continued stating herself as psychologist and pedagogue. Some of her followers wanted her to share the photo of her diploma, but she didn't share. The claims are reinforced by this situation, on the other hand didn't clarified. Some of her followers believed her, some others didn't and rejected. Although there is a doubt about her education, she is still very popular. Like showing sympathies, showing hate can be very extreme to popular virtual identities. On Instagram and YouTube, people write comments such as "you look terrible and horrible", "you are unskilled and unqualified", "you use your child to earn money", "you don't have a right and capacity to talk about child development".

Feelings of the people determine acceptance and rejection on social media. Other sample groups are fashion-make up bloggers and females who are sharing food recipes. Both of the groups are very popular on Instagram and YouTube in Turkey. Fashion and make up bloggers have many followers on social media. People follow them in order to keep with the fashion and make up. Most of the women buy the clothes bloggers wear and make up products bloggers recommend. This demonstrates they trust bloggers' advices and taste of fashion. They ask questions about the brand of bloggers' clothes and make up products. Many young adults and teenagers try to wear like bloggers and imitate those popular bloggers' style. Although every woman is different from each other when their appearance and body shapes are considered, they try to dress in the same way as bloggers do. Moreover, every woman has different type of skin, so they need to choose make up products according to their skin type. When they see a product from the bloggers, they just want to use that product without thinking about their skin type. Although women pay too much attention to their appearance and skin, they just trust advices of the bloggers without thinking about their body shapes and skin type. Women ask many questions and write comments on bloggers' accounts. They ask questions as a comment such as "I have a dry skin, can you recommend me some products for dry skin?", "I am blonde, which tones of colors should I use for my make up?" or "can you tell me the products that you use for skin protecting?".

Food recipes shared on Instagram and YouTube also highly accepted by many women. There are Instagram accounts and YouTube channels that females share food recipes. They have many followers and most of them are women again. Their recipes are tried by a lot of followers and after trial of a recipe, they send photos of the foods. Even though they don't know the person who is sharing food recipes, women try those recipes without any doubt. If they understand the recipe well, they don't ask any question while trying the recipe and they send photos after cooking. Answers of the participants indicate acceptance or rejection directly. Interview done with 10 participants consist of both mothers and university students. 6 of them are mothers graduated from university, the rest 4 participants are university students. 3 of the participants don't know Internet Mothers, the rest 6 participants know Internet Mothers and also follow on social media. Those 6 women who follow Internet Mothers are mothers in real life, the rest 4 who don't follow Internet mothers are university students. Only one of the university students know Internet Mother, but don't follow on social media. All of the 6 mothers claimed that they are following Internet mothers in order to inform about child development and hear about social activities for their children. The reason for other 4 people who don't follow Internet mothers stated they don't interested in children. In addition to this, one of 4 participants complained about Internet Mothers because she thinks they are trying to share every moment of their children and ignore privacy. 7 of the participants follow fashion and make up bloggers on social media.

All of them follow bloggers because they interested in and inform about fashion and make up products. They also remark that they are trying the products bloggers advised. 3 out of 10 participants don't follow bloggers because they thought bloggers are just advertising the products and get profit from them. Moreover, those 3 participants also claimed that the products bloggers recommended cannot be suitable and appropriate for all types of body shapes and skin types. For the women who are sharing food recipes on Instagram and YouTube, 3 of the participants don't follow, the rest follow and try the recipes. Those 3 participants indicated they are not cooking in their daily lives and not interested in cooking. The rest 7 people follow, 6 of them are mothers and they are cooking in their daily lives, other one participant is university student and interested in cooking. Last question asked to the participants is whether they have similarities with the people they follow or not. Only 2 of the participants claimed that they don't have any similarities, because they find the things attractive that they don't have and belong. Other 8 participants who follow those popular virtual identities think they have similarities between them and the people they follow, that's why they follow. In summary, the results of interview demonstrate people follow and accept popular virtual identities according to their similarities and interests. The group people belong according to their similarities and interests lead them to accept or reject virtual identities.

Discussion and Results

Collected data for this paper give the results of the reasons why people accept or reject popular virtual identities on social media. According to the data of this paper, acceptance and trust come from the similarities between users and the people they follow on Instagram and YouTube. This result refers to the Social Identity Theory which claims concept of the self comes from the groups that person belongs. People have a tendency to accept and trust virtual identities which they have similarities or they are in the same groups. For instance, mothers accept and believe Internet Mothers because they are the members of same group, "mothers". They are mothers and take care of their children in common. Strong points of the paper are interview and observed social media comments support the main idea and hypothesis of this paper. Target group and their answers are appropriate for data and reinforce the theory. The results of the interview may not be accurate exactly, because there are limited participants for observation and interview. Results may be change according to the number of the participants, also age, gender, social status, social environment can have an impact on the results. People's feelings towards popular virtual identities are not consistent and sustainable. Acceptance and rejection of those virtual identities may change in some cases. They live their lives in front of their followers, they share every moment of their lives with their families or friends on social media. If they do something morally inappropriate, their followers may change their behaviors and feelings from acceptance to rejection. Their followers pay too much attention to their ideas and behaviors on social media. For instance, if popular people on social media support campaigns done for animals, animal lovers may start to like and accept them. So, feelings and behaviors towards popular virtual identities can change accordingly some behaviors and statements of these identities. For this reason, results of the interview and observed social media comments may not reflect the exact and permanent situation in social media.

Conclusion

As mentioned above, social media has already become a significant part of people's lives with the development of technology and the Internet. In this Internet-oriented world, almost everybody has virtual identities beside their physical identities. In Turkey, there are popular virtual identities which are Internet Mothers, fashion-make up bloggers and women who are sharing food recipes. All of those virtual identities have many followers on Instagram and YouTube, in addition to this they gained too much trust from many people. Many of their followers believe everything they say and take too much care about their advices. On the other hand, some people strictly reject them and criticize because those virtual identities don't have enough knowledge to talk about some specific issues. The most popular virtual identities are Internet Mothers in Turkey now. Their followers consult Internet Mothers in order to inform about child development and mother issues. This is a surprising situation because people prefer Internet Mothers to inform about their children, rather than psychologists and pedagogues. This high level of trust gives rise to question which is whether these virtual identities are lying or not. Because almost all of those virtual identities didn't take education about psychology, child development, fashion-make up and cooking. This is double sided question because some people are consulting those virtual identities without any doubt, but some others blame them as they are lying. The reason for both acceptance and rejection may be the social identities of individuals. People are more likely to follow they have similarities, not to follow they don't have any similarities. Their interest, social environment, social identity, groups they belong in their physical lives affect acceptance or rejection on social media.

Acknowledgement

This paper was written within the scope of the undergraduate course "Advanced Issues in Communication Studies" (Fall 2017-2018) of the Department of Communication and Design at Bilkent University which was directed by Dr. Dr. Lutz Peschke.

References

Latané, Bibb (1981): The Psychology of Social Impact. *American Psychologists*, 36. 343-356. http://psycnet.apa.org/record/1982-01296-001 Accessed on Apr. 10, 2018.

McLeod, Saul (2008): Social Identity Theory. *Simply Psychology*. Retrieved from https://www.simplypsychology.org/social-identity-theory.html Accessed on Apr. 10, 2018.

Rowe, Jonathan: Social Impact Theory. Retrieved from http://www.psychologywizard.net/social-impact-theory-ao1-ao2-ao3.html [last access:]

Vallor, Shannon (2016): Social Networking and Ethics, *The Stanford Encyclopedia of Philosophy (Winter 2016 Edition)*. Retrieved from https://plato.stanford.edu/entries/ethics-social-networking/ Accessed on Apr. 10, 2018.

Tajfel, Henri / Turner, John C. (2004): The Social Identity Theory of Intergroup Behavior. In: Jost, John T./Sidanius, Jim (eds.), *Key readings in social psychology. Political psychology: Key readings* (pp. 276-293). New York, NY, US: Psychology Press. Retrieved from http://psycnet.apa.org/record/2004-13697-016 Accessed on Apr. 10, 2018.

Snapchat Use and Its Effect on Young People
The Potential of Cyberbullying Through the Use of Application

Damla Gürkanlı*

Abstract

The Internet holds tremendous potential for advancement. It gives an uncommon volume of assets for data and learning that opens new open doors and difficulties for expression and interest. 'Fighting words' also appear on smartphones in the hands of people on both sides of a heated confrontation but now we also live in cyberspace. Social media operate in parallel with crowd dynamics in the street. "Fighting words" may be in the air, but they will also appear on smartphones in the hands of people on both sides of a heated confrontation. This mix is yet to be reckoned with by the law. Vanishing photograph and video messages are Snapchat's charm, and have been around any longer than Instagram's form Snapchat has the upside of straightforwardness: You communicate something specific, somebody takes a gander at it, and it's gone and same goes for private messages as well. The discussion sticks around for a couple of messages, however if you close the discussion or quit the application, those messages will vanish also. That is an immense in addition, and what's made Snapchat so famous throughout the years. The application's primary offering point is the thing that makes it the ideal play area for digital harassers to rule. While this is occurring on various stages, instinctively, some may state Snapchat is an extremely encouraging stage for individuals with disdainful, frightful motivation, who need to escape with no proof being deserted. Now and then people who are harassed are fairly protected from the strategies through which

---

* Damla Gürkanlı, Bilkent University, Department of Communication and Design. Ankara/Turkey

oppressors' favor. In any case, with Snapchat being such a well-known device, to the point that pretty much every adolescent is utilizing, it makes it a perfect approach to target people. The individuals who are harassed regularly need to end up plainly more prominent, and they may feel they can do as such by utilizing this application. They will probably either utilize looser security settings or acknowledge more individuals as companions trying to develop their fame. The purpose of the present study is to examine the intensity of use of social networks by individuals and the cases of cyberbullying / victimization. Pre-test for survey, related and relevant legal themes about the application were explained and qualitatively examined.

Key Words: Freedom of speech, bullying, Snapchat, cyber mobbing.

Introduction

Alongside the Internet infiltrating our lives immediately, stereotyped structures have started to change. Outstanding amongst other cases of this is our social relations. Because of the worldwide structure of the Internet, we can without much of a stretch speak with many individuals we know or don't have the foggiest idea. Particularly as of late, one might say that long range interpersonal communication locales are the most famous and clever structures utilized on the web. The Internet is a noteworthy procedure in today's world. Truth be told, interpersonal organizations that enable web clients to speak with their companions, share different video, photograph and status data may not generally be utilized for their proposed purposes. Harassing conduct has made diverse ideas by consolidating with the virtual world. The utilization of data and correspondence advances to hurt others is characterized as digital tormenting (Belsey 2004). A Canadian analyst Bill Belsey who is the primary individual who is using the word cyberbullying. This idea, which entered the writing as digital harassing, has been portrayed by a few specialists (ibid.) as an alternate type of animosity or conventional tormenting, and by a few analysts (Juvonen/Gross 2008) has a totally extraordinary structure from harassing as far as structure and size.) Digital harassing, while at the same time being comparable in its purpose to hurt others through power and control, is diverse because of the utilization of these new advances and applications like Snapchat. Snapchat is an application accessible on the most widespread smartphone systems. It can send writings, photographs, or recordings which are accessible for up to 10 seconds. Following 10 seconds the picture or video is erased from the telephone and the organization's servers. Since Snapchat stories vanish following 24 hours, the substance is crude and unscripted, permitting your image message to emerge and have a bona fide voice. In this paper it has been asked, Snapchat use has the potential of cyberbullying and abuses using application?

While the Internet becomes an integral part of people's lives. One has propensity to use the Internet's limitless platform and reach all kinds of information. While harassing has already been constrained to face to face experiences, it has now stretched out to on the web and diverse ways. Güneş Peschke (2016) defines freedom of speech as follows "According to the provision of Article 26 of our Constitution; everyone, expressions of opinions and opinions by words, writing, pictures or other means, alone or in aggregate, and the right to disseminate " Starting from this definition, expressing that flexibility of articulation and opportunity of press are rights which can struggle with each other, so here and the utilization of the flexibility of press and opportunity of articulation, singular rights can be disregarded (ibid.: 30). SnapChat is one of the quickest developing thing among youngsters, making it the perfect place for mobbers to focus on their casualties. This photo and video content choice enables people to send a photo or short video to one or a few companions. The photo or video that is sent is just accessible on the receiver's telephone for a brief timeframe, up to 10 seconds. Presently, the picture or video is erased from the telephone and the servers. These actualities make the application the ideal chance to utilize new digital tormenting strategies to assault their victims and bully them.

The greatest attract to utilizing Snapchat as a digital harassing system is the way that photos and recordings vanish inside 10 seconds in the wake of being seen. Bullies would prefer not to leave any proof of what they are doing at the danger of being gotten. They feel if the photo or video they send vanishes before the harassing casualty can demonstrate it to a grown-up, they are free. Generally, this makes this application ideal setting for digital harassers. Most teenagers don't know how to catch a screen shot of the photo or don not have the common sense to do as such seemingly out of the moment. Commonly, spooks get a kick out of the chance to get whatever number individuals required as could reasonably be expected.

Tragically, despite the fact that casualties do not frequently have the common sense to make a screenshot to get the domineering jerk stuck in an unfortunate situation, the individuals who are doing the digital harassing regularly know how. In these circumstances, on the off chance that they get their hands on a humiliating photo of another understudy, they may take a brisk depiction on their mobile phone and afterward keep on passing it around. It was discovered that people who utilize long range interpersonal communication destinations as often as possible have more cyberbullying and digital casualties than the individuals who utilize less (Tuncer / Dikmen 2016). In these circumstances, on the off chance that they get their hands on a humiliating photo of another understudy, they may take a speedy preview on their mobile phone and afterward keep on passing it around. Despite the fact that Snapchat is intended to be utilized with pictures, there are different ways spooks can use to assault their casualties. Sending humiliating photographs or photographs that appear to contrast the casualty with a creature or another defamatory thing can frequently be a successful approach to assaulting the other individual. Be that as it may, this isn't the main way this application can be utilized to assault. A few people make recordings that have words on them and send those through the application.

The general belief is that "what's the damage the photo is gone in 10 seconds." But that is not generally the situation. While the pictures vanish from the application itself, there's nothing incorporated with the application to stop kids on the less than desirable end from taking a screen shot and sparing it or utilizing another gadget to take a photo of their mobile phone screen. There are even a few hacks that use the telephone's screenshot abilities and the multitasking bar. Be that as it may, this new Snapchat "hack," divulged by website specialist and undergrad Raj Vir and first gave an account of by TechCrunch, is said to enable clients to "effortlessly spare screenshots of 'snaps' in a couple of basic strides, without any than Snapchat and your multitasking bar." These screenshots can clearly be taken furtively, without the sender discovering. Furthermore, an enormous number of photographs are shared each day on Snapchat. In any case, the interest to adolescents isn't the photograph sharing ability however that those photographs naturally self-destruct in ten seconds or less. Or, on the other hand, so they think.

Therefore, a few adolescents utilize Snapchat to share unseemly or bare photographs of themselves or others supposing it will be gone in ten seconds in any case.

Since Snapchat's improvement however, a few hacks have surfaced enabling children to spare or take screenshots of the photographs. This implies the photographs never genuinely vanish. Subsequently, kids some of the time spare the photographs and later post them freely to humiliate and embarrass the sender. Interpersonal organizations are evident supporter of cyberbullying, yet it is difficult to just accuse innovation or informal communities for teenager suicide due to digital mobbing. It would not exist without person's cooperation there was a harassing before interpersonal organization. Bekker (1963): "Deviation isn't a sort of activity, but instead the consequence of utilizing authorizations and principles by others" So, the inquiry "who and how characterizes the deviation" is methodologically essential clarifying the wonder of digital harassing. The impression of typical and degenerate conduct is in accordance with the social setting and shifts between nations on account of social, logical and monetary contrasts Durkheim's hypothesis is figured by four sorts of suicide (Egoistic, Altruistic, Anomic, and Fatalistic) that are portrayed by the levels of social combination and social control a man encounters.

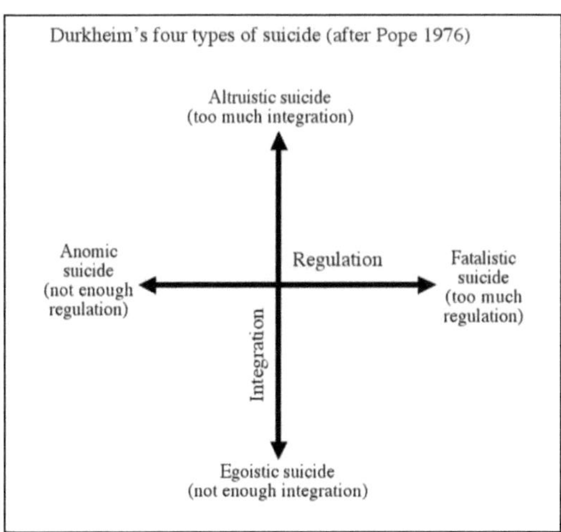

Figure 1: Émile Durkheim's theory of suicide breannaray. Source: wordpress.com (Zevallos 2007)

The perception of normal and deviant behavior is in line with the social context and varies between countries because of cultural, contextual and economic differences Durkheim's theory is formulated by four types of suicide (Egoistic, Altruistic, Anomic, and Fatalistic) that are described by the levels of social integration and social regulation a person's experiences. In outrageous cases, digital tormenting can be related with Durkheim's hypothesis of self-absorbed suicide. As per Durkheim prideful suicide ends up noticeably show when a man feels socially disengaged from society and feels he or she has no place in the public eye. The individual may likewise feel a feeling of useless or despondency, this more often than not happens when the level of social joining is low. People that experience digital tormenting are typically debilitated; mortified or bugged by and large the individual may abstain from looking for help and in a few conditions, they can take their own life. Suicides caused by digital tormenting are related with Durkheim's hypothesis of proud suicide in light of the fact that the individual being harassed is normally ousted from the social gathering. Digital tormenting, "infection" as the illness spreads the watcher can see the symptoms. This example exhibits how quick the infection spreads and contaminates others and can demolish the lives of its casualties, in this case from every angle Tovonna Holton, 15, was a beautiful young lady with a brilliant future in front of her at Wiregrass Ranch High School in Wesley Chapel, Florida. Yet, the majority of that changed a weekend ago when a video of her cleaning up at school without her insight was coursed utilizing Snapchat by mean schoolmates. Her mom, Levon Holton-Teamer, saw that her girl was vexed and at first did not think about the video and the digital tormenting that her little girl was experiencing. As per her mom she expressed, "'Mommy, I owe them; I owe them." Tovonna took her mom's firearm from her handbag, without her insight, and finished her life.

In this segment, for the arrangement of the examination issue, Results are indicated by the discoveries acquired and clarifications are composed. By definition, tormenting and cyberbullying are subjective -

implying that everyone has an alternate thought of which practices qualify as being harsh. Nonetheless, there is a general accord of online practices that are considered to fall inside the transmit of cyberbullying. Snapchat's ten second and disappeared makes it both less demanding, and more troublesome for cyberbullies. It enables them to take implicating photographs, occasionally without the casualty notwithstanding acknowledging it, and send badgering without confirm enduring sufficiently long to be followed. Nevertheless, with speedy information of how to take a screenshot, a casualty can track provocation, and there's an approach to stop the assault of consistent messages.

Snapchat has group of rules, for example, no erotic entertainment, and ensuring somebody's protection, for example, not taking pics without another person's learning. What's more, Snapchat's approach is no screenshots, despite them against tormenting position. It's a confused field. In any case, they likewise have an announcing territory; yet additionally prescribe a piece first arrangement. Snapchat has arrangements to ensure client's security, and to avoid harassing. Essentially, to anticipate cyberbullying, they don't take into consideration intrusions of protection, for example, taking snaps of others without their insight. Moreover, they don't take into consideration pantomime, much like YouTube, which implies making counterfeit records, even to mimic superstars. At long last, they have a strict no-badgering approach, which implies once somebody has blocked you, you may not keep on harassing them from another record, or from another record. Their no-nakedness approach, particularly for those under 18 can add to a no-tormenting condition by not considering humiliating substance, since it even precludes sexually unequivocal illustrations on generally amiable snaps.

Statistics show the results of a survey conducted by Cint on the distribution of social media used in Turkey in 2016 and 2017. In 2017, 24.47 percent of respondents stated that they use Facebook. Despite the decrease seen among survey respondents, social networks in Turkey** are generally increasing their reach. (Statista, 2017) This measurement demonstrates the consequences of a review directed by Cint on the conveyance of online networking utilized as a part of Turkey in 2016 and 2017. In 2017, 24.47 percent of respondents expressed that they utilize Facebook. Despite the reduction seen among overview respondents, informal organizations in Turkey** are by and large expanding their span. By 2021, the interpersonal organization entrance rate is anticipated to achieve 52.55 percent, up from 40.69 percent in 2015. Facebook alone is required to achieve 51.31 percent** of the Turkish populace by 2012, having expanded from a rate of 39.48 percent in 2015. At the point when taken a gander at, after some time, from 2007, through 2016, the rate of detailed cyberbullying guilty parties has declined strongly from 19.1% to 12.0% of understudies revealing self-announcing; be that as it may, the rates likewise vary altogether from year to year, in some cases as much as 5-7%. Cyberbullying.org orders information from ten unique examinations to assemble a normal of about 15.8% understudies who detailed cyberbullying others, over the 9-year contemplate period, with a low of 11.5% announcing in 2009, with a particularly low example class measure. Intriguingly, exploitation rates are almost doubled the self-detailing rates for spooks, which proposes that either spooks are tormenting more than one casualty, that casualties feel imperious by activities that domineering jerks don't really feel is harassing, or that domineering jerks are under-revealing. What's more, not at all like the disordered ascent and fall of the cyber-mobbing self-announcing, exploitation rates appear on an enduring move since 2007, except for two slight dunks in 2010 and 2013. The normal revealing rate for casualties, arranged more than ten investigations from cyberbullying.org is 27.9% and incorporates digital harassing in all structures, for example, email, in the classroom, and over other electronic media.

Digital harassing can be portrayed as forceful, deliberate exercises performed by an individual or a social event of people by methods for automated particular methodologies, for instance, sending messages and posting comments against a loss. Not the same as standard tormenting that as a rule happens at school in the midst of very close correspondence. Digital tormenting does not seem to segregate for sex. Not at all like different sorts of tormenting where, for instance, physical hostility is more normally connected with guys, and social animosity is all the more commonly connected with females, digital harassing is even more similarly disseminated. The two sexes have all the earmarks of being similarly connected with digital harassing practices. The disassociated association with screens makes it simpler for the two sexual orientations to connect with practices that they may not generally take part in, in the event that they were looked with an individual, making it less demanding for the two sexes to take part in digital harassing practices; it resembles it's at the same time incident to both a genuine, and a not-authentic individual.

With the extending noticeable quality of uses applications, computerized tormenting has ascended as a troublesome issue annoying children and young adults. Past examinations of advanced bugging focused on wide audits and its psychological outcomes for losses, and were essentially driven by social scientists and experts. Accordingly, casualties of cyberbullying are additionally, generally, similarly spread among sex. There's a marginally bigger number of revealed lifetime female digital harasser casualties, however by and large, casualties are similarly spread amongst male and female, particularly among intermediate school community. As per cyberbullying.org, center schoolers utilize the Internet for a wide assortment of purposes, and in slipping request, it's as a matter of first importance for web based recreations and homework, and ultimately for visit rooms.

Pretesting is the way toward uniting individuals from the need group of onlookers to respond to the parts of a correspondence crusade before they are created in conclusive frame. Pre-testing measures the response of the chose gathering of people and decides if the need crowd will discover the segments - as a rule draft material justifiable, authentic and engaging. Pre-test for survey is utilized as a part of this paper by influencing review to consider which comprises of the following questions. The primary questions are the normal every day using time of the web, the age, the frequency of using social networks to decide if they use social network and snapchat. The following inquiries are about sorts of bullying and whether they are harassed or not, and which of the given materials are cyberbullying and six questions were given for this reason.

As per the chart appeared in Figure 2 (10%) of the respondents are use social media rarely. 1 (10%) respondents use social media consistently. These groups which is not use social media so often have never experienced cyberbullying. What's more, 8 (80%) of the respondents are using social media frequently. As it can be seen in Figure 3, 4 (%44,44) say 'yes', 5(%55,56) 'no'. As can be seen in results, When the distribution of the answers they see is examined,(80%) of the respondents in the virtual environment threatening to publish or publish pictures or videos, 5 (50%) people or persons To send a large number of e-mails, 5 of them (50%) were not able to communicate with people we did not know on social networks 3 of them(30%) of people or persons are to be thrown out of online games, 10 of them (100%) by hiding the identity in the virtual environment or by impersonating a different person are trying to learn the private information, 2 of them (20%)requests to send a friend request that you do not recognize on social networks.

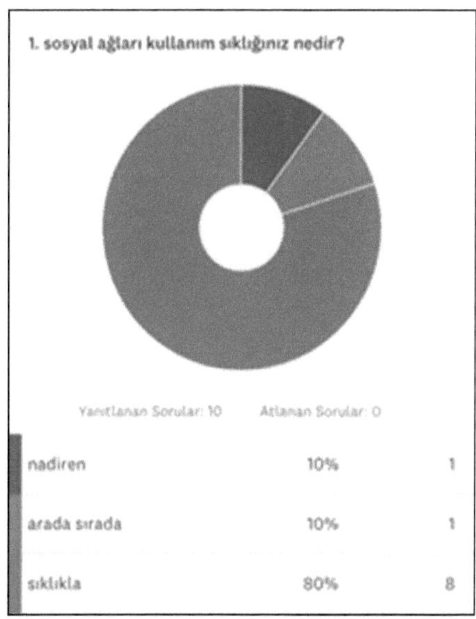

Figure 2: How often do you use social media? (Retrieved from https://tr.surveymonkey.com/

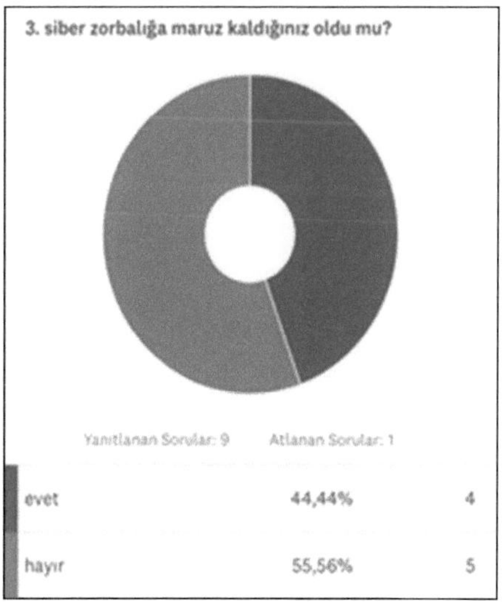

Figure 3: have you ever been exposed to cyberbullying (Retrieved from https://tr.surveymonkey.com/)

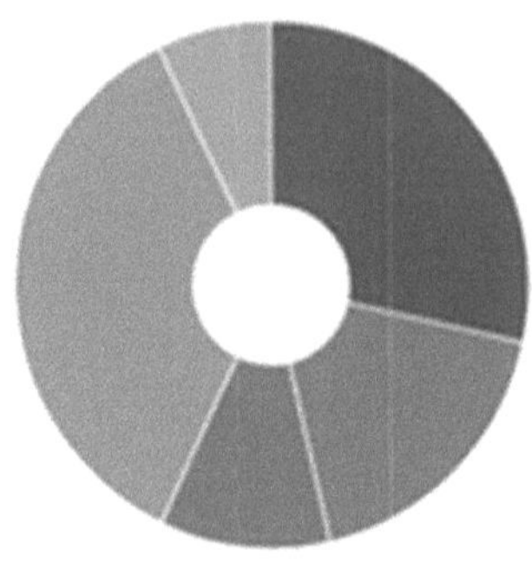

Figure 4: Which of these actions could be considered as cyber-bullying for you?
(Retrieved from https://tr.surveymonkey.com/)

Pretesting can anticipate issues like these. It guarantees that materials pass on a reasonable and powerful message about liquor, tobacco, and different medications to a program's intended interest group. It causes me Select message ideas - styles, arrangements, representative, and advances, (for example, fear, humor, sympathy) "Pretesting" is significant at a few phases of message and material improvement. Results can be utilized in this paper. Of the beginning times to test ideas or general issues and to start thoughts; different kind of questions are more helpful when materials are in near definite frame.

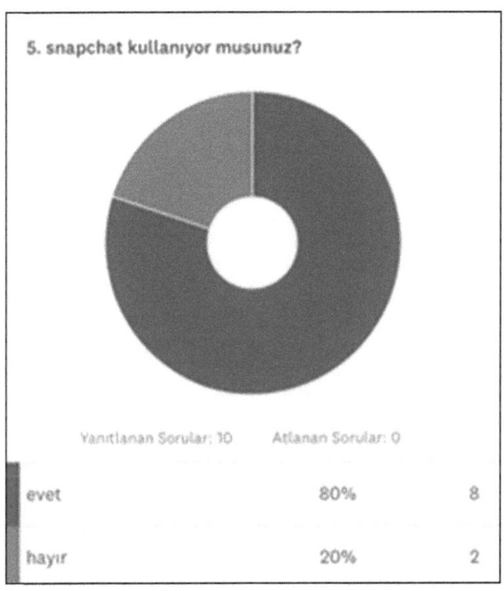

Figure 5: Do you use Snapchat? (Retrieved from https://tr.surveymonkey.com/

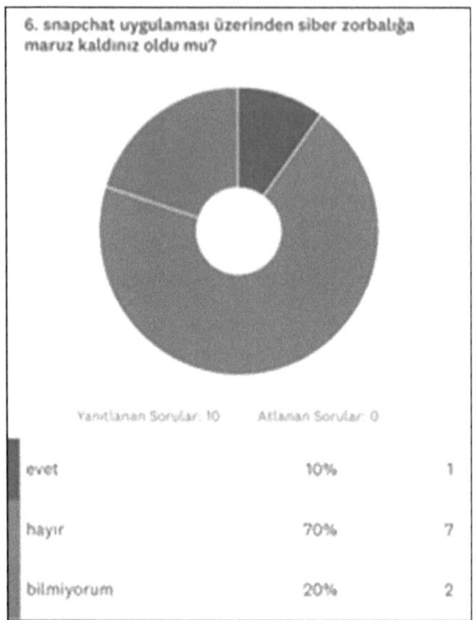

Figure 6: Have you ever been exposed mobbing? (Retrieved from
https://tr.surveymonkey.com/

Also 8 (%80) say yes to using Snapchat other 2 (%20) say no. 1 (%10)
have been exposed to cyber-mobbing through Snapchat 7 (%80) of them
have never been expose 2 (%20) of them do not know.

Conclusion

Increased upgrades in science and advancement over the span of the
latest couple of years have impacted our lives from various perspectives.
Advancement has begun to have its spot in our lives without being
somewhat, colossal individual; even a new-born child who has not yet
tended to talk is from every angle using mobile phones effortlessly.
Along these lines, it is inevitable that a couple of practices in our lives are
epitomized in different courses with advancement. Web and individual
to individual correspondence areas used together with development
empower us to grant paying little mind to whether we have low

probability of encountering in our lives. The way that casual association districts have various positive edges, (for instance, video or voice talking) makes it possible to use them in significant sums in a short time period. Nevertheless, it similarly exhibits that tormenting rehearses, for instance, hate, shock, hate, and requital that are inherent in individuals will moreover be seen on these phases in the opposite. As the repeat of casual group utilize augments in the revelations of the examination, it is seen that the general population are displayed to all the additionally cyberbullying. It is continually advantageous to cover a man's identity on the Internet. A delineation would be for individuals who might lean toward not to reveal their identity on casual groups to open fraud records.

Right when individuals are looked far as tormenting earnestness, it can be seen that these opposite practices can be depicted in an extensive variety of ways. In any case, it is an intriguing finding that individuals are found to have such a strange condition of prologue to direct with computerized tormenting. As demonstrated by this situation, it is lacking to use the information that individuals have when they enter the web condition. To rehearse practices that will grow acknowledgments and thoughtfulness regarding annoying. Workshops can be given to keep the computerized tormenting conditions from spreading on relational associations and to engage individuals to secure their own information in this condition. It should be indicated that the Special Scope can establish the framework for the weakness, inadequacy and deficiencies of being conferred to others through casual groups. Moreover, mind should be taken not to sign in to a casual association account on a non-PC.

Acknowledgement

This paper was written within the scope of the undergraduate course "Advanced Issues in Communication Studies" (Fall 2017-2018) of the Department of

Communication and Design at Bilkent University which was directed by Dr. Dr. Lutz Peschke.

References

Cyber Bullying: Helping the Bullied, Stopping the Bullies. (n.d.). Retrieved December 19, 2017, from http://backgroundchecks.org/cyber-bullying-helping-the-bullied-stopping-the-bullies.html

Education, Children's Rights and the EU. (n.d.). Children and the European Union: Rights, Welfare and Accountability. doi:10.5040/9781472566133.ch-006

Graphics (n.d.). Retrieved from https://tr.surveymonkey.com/

Güneş Peschke, Seldağ (2014): Roma Hukukundan Günümüze Kişilik Haklarının Korunması. Ankara: Yetkin.

Güneş Peschke, Seldağ (2016): Privacy v. Freedom of Press: The Current Legal developments in Turkey. *Law and Justice Review*, 7 (12), 1-13.

Hmissa, W. / Zempinski, J. (2017). Http://www.fgcu.edu/Aquila/files/3-2_Hmissa_et_al_Environmental_Surface_Sampling_for_Methicillin_Resistant_Staphylococcus_aureus_(MRSA).pdf. *Aquila: The FGCU Student Research Journal*, 3(2). doi:10.24049/aq.3.2.7Home. (n.d.). Retrieved December 19, 2017, from https://cyberbullying.org/

Http://ljournal.ru/wp-content/uploads/2017/03/a-2017-023.pdf. (2017). doi:10.18411/a-2017-023

Roof, K. (2014, May 13). Mark Cuban Takes on Snapchat with Cyber Dust. Retrieved December 19, 2017, from http://www.foxbusiness.com/features/2014/05/13/mark-cuban-takes-on-snapchat-with-cyber-dust.html (n.d.). Retrieved December 19, 2017, from http://webshells.com/spantrans/etica.htm

SnapChat Bullying Tactics. (2014, September 25). Retrieved December 19, 2017, from http://nobullying.com/snapchat-bullying-tactics/

Snapchat launches #BeStrong filter to help stop cyberbullying - BBC Newsbeat. (2015, November 18). Retrieved December 19, 2017, from http://www.bbc.co.uk/newsbeat/article/34853591/snapchat-launches-bestrong-filter-to-help-stop-cyberbullying

Suicide. (n.d.). Retrieved from

https://breannaray.files.wordpress.com/2014/12/bd6e2-suicide.jpg?w=243&h=206

The Deal with Snapchat Safety. (2014, November 05). Retrieved December 19, 2017, from http://nobullying.com/can-you-use-snapchat-safely/

Turkey: Social media usage 2016-2017 | Survey. Retrieved December 21, 2017, from https://www.statista.com/statistics/570098/distribution-of-social-media-used-turkey/

Utz Sonja / Muscanell, Nicole / Cameran, Khalid (2015): Snapchat elicits more

jealousy than Facebook: A comparison of Snapchat and Facebook use. *Cyberpsychology, Behavior, and Social Networking, 18*(3), 141–146. doi:10.1089/cyber.2014.0479

What is Cyber Storm? - Definition from WhatIs.com. (n.d.). Retrieved December 19, 2017, from http://searchsecurity.techtarget.com/definition/Cyber-Storm

Zhao, R., & Mao, K. (2017). Cyberbullying Detection Based on Semantic-Enhanced Marginalized Denoising Auto-Encoder. *IEEE Transactions on Affective Computing,8*(3), 328-339. doi:10.1109/taffc.2016.25316

PART II:
ONLINE COMMUNICATION BETWEEN
CORPORATE COMMUNICATION AND NEW
BUSINESS STRATEGIES

Evolution of Television
Rise of Video-on-Demand Services in Cases of Amazon Prime & Netflix

Can Gürmeriç[*]

1. Introduction

Smartphones, computers and internet; the perception of our lives have changed in the 21st Century by these technological advancements. Business life, entertainment and education are some of the examples which undergo a radical change over the last two decades. Now, media have classified under two categories; traditional and new. New media uses internet with traditional media elements, and by that new and emerging products of media have been created. This research will focus on video on demand services, which are platforms that combine television, cinema and internet. By monthly or yearly subscriptions, users have the benefit of watching thousands of video materials with high definition quality via internet. These services could be used via tablets, smartphones, computers and smart televisions with internet connectivity. By subscribing to a plan and downloading the application of the video on demand service, users can watch television series, movies and other visual material without limits. Contrary to traditional television, these platforms do not put advertisements between products, the experience remains uninterrupted.

Convergence of different systems like internet, mobile devices and computers, force television into a change. By that force, television faces

[*] Can Gürmeriç, Bilkent University, Department of Communication and Design. Ankara/Turkey

a remediation which is changing the medium, audience, the content. Viewing habits are also changing along with the other elements. Video-on-Demand services like Netflix and Amazon Prime combines current trends in the media inside a single platform. By focusing on the current condition of the traditional television with theories and researches, an analysis will be made in order to project the future for the television. Preceding of the television like other media elements, is likely be digital and online. The purpose of this research is to show the significance of new media and internet over the medium and its components, audience and content.

1.1 Abstract

This research paper analyzes the phenomenon of internet based subscription Video-on-Demand services and compare it with the traditional television (Cable TV, Satellite, Linear Television) medium. By technological advancements and improvements, most of the services and media elements have been changing. With computers, smartphones and internet, media has gone through a radical change. New media today is a part of the daily life and because of the convergence of different technologies and media elements, it is changing constantly. With the improvements in the traditional media, remediation happens as a consequence. Television is also in between this convergence and remediation. Video-on-Demand services are the results of internet and digitization. With the rise of these platforms, traditional television viewership has been decreasing. In this paper, the current status of television medium, the success of Video-on-Demand services and future of television medium will be analyzed with the help of media theories, researches and statistics. By that, possible factors which might affect the rise of Video-on-Demand services will be presented and by that data, some deductions about the future of television medium will be made accordingly.

1.2 Research Questions

- RQ1: Are Subscription based Video-On-Demand services overcoming traditional television in the industry?

- RQ2: What are the factors effecting the success of Video-On-Demand platforms?

- RQ3: What could be the future of television medium?

1.3 Literature Review

To understand the current status of television, the historical steps and the development of the medium should be analyzed first. By combining historical events and their reflections on the television Lundgren (2015) analyzes the direction of the television today. In Peters' review, (2000) same approach was used to show the evolution of the television. With technological developments, the perception of television has not radically changed; but evolved in time by the needs of the mass audience.

By the proliferation of DVR devices and Pay TV systems; the linearity of the television started to change. These are the events that started the birth of streaming services or video-on-demand industry in the first place. In the analysis of Kovacs, (2015) the steps led to the streaming services are analyzed. By the new systems that challenge the linear and traditional status of the television; the audience and the content started to change. Kovacs investigated the evolution of streaming services by focusing on Netflix and Netflix's strategies. The industry created by the streaming services started to expand increasingly after 2005. By looking to the statistics, Kovacs have made some predictions about the industry for the short and medium terms. LaPorte (2014) in the other hand, started the analysis in the DVD age. The transformation from the DVD to internet streaming concept is observed by looking to the strategies used by Netflix. It is shown that content produced and the strategies by the Netflix are collinear; and always changing by the demand and the events that effect the industry. The success of the Netflix is that mechanism consequently.

In order to understand the change in the medium of television, previous media theories must be visited. Terms like convergence and remediation are important when analyzing the effects of technological developments to the television and media in general. Convergence means a merging of two separate elements; and forming a unique new one. Canavilhas (2012) explained the convergence process in television by comparing the medium to other media elements. The digital and the traditional agents of these elements are gradually become closer to form new mediums. Also, Canavilhas stated that the convergence could not be seen separately in television or a different medium; but it is a process that evolving gradually in all of the media agents. Remediation on the other hand means improvement. Bolter, (1999) interpreted the technological changes in the media as a remediation of an existing medium, rather than changing radically. The steps of remediation were analyzed by looking at the content, production and the projection.

Doyle (2016) in his analysis about video-on-demand services, focused on the digitization's effect on television medium. The distribution and the consumption of the new television industry clarified with a negative attitude for the technological changes. Doyle stated the video-on-demand services are only in the business for money; not for the content or the improvement for the medium. Mazzoli (2015) also approaches the matter with a similar attitude. The current status of the television is described as "Post TV" which is a convergence of internet and the television. But Mazzoli states some concerns about the power and the control of that new mechanism. By giving the power of monitoring behavior of the audience for production; eventually these companies could use this power in order to surveil the public accordingly.

There are different approaches to the new status of the television which is combined with the video-on-demand services. Mahanti (2014) states that the streaming services' ability to change linearity, the content of the television material will also change. "Binge-watching" term is used to express multiple content viewing successively. By the behavioral changes in the viewing, the content will be changed accordingly. Fontaine (2013) also approaches the matter similarly. Fontaine shoes the connection between audience, demand, prices, content and the advertisements all together; forming a new and interactive organism which will eventually decide on the future of the television. Bulck & Enli (2010) also states the non-linear form of the new television will change the content accordingly. Another similar is from Lee & Lee. (1995) By monitoring the audience behavior, authors deduced that interactive television will change the future of television. The change will happen in content, audience and in the medium itself. Einav and Carey (2009) approaches the matter likewise. By the changes in the medium, the perception of television has changed in every way; from content, to audience, to viewing behaviors. Einav and Carey states that even the size or resolution of the television have an important effect over the medium. Urriciho states in his article (2005) that the technological changes create a flow of content which will affect the consumption behavior of the audience and also the content. By that change, the culture of the television will eventually change according to his opinion. Also in parallel with Mazzoli, presents some concerns about the privacy and security by the power of the new medium.

One of the factors affecting the success of the video-on-demand services is the lack of advertisements compared to the traditional television. Gonzales (2015) states in his article that, media conglomerates are actually decreasing commercial lengths to compete with the streaming services. By decreasing, media channels aim to increase the effect of advertisements. Advertisements are important agents for the traditional television and by the streaming services; the phenomenon started to change as well as the content.

The consumer driven structure of streaming services is different than the traditional television medium as well. Sharma (2013) states the unique material production by the Netflix and Amazon Prime. By surveys, feedbacks and ratings; these companies decide on the future of their content with the direct effect of the audience. In a way audience and the content becomes one. This unique concept also challenges the traditional television's structure of top-to-down mechanism as well. The importance of reviews and ratings by the users is also analyzed by Baugher & Ramos. (2016) In the research, it is found out that there is a direct relation of Amazon ratings of certain movies with the sales of the products. Combining a relatively old element like a DVD and the internet; Baugher & Ramos shows the importance of audience and the consumer-driven structure of new media once more.

By looking to the statistical data Nielsen (2014) come up that the audience has the control over the content in the new media system of television and internet. The correlation of mobile device usage, internet usage between the video-on-demand services is shown by the research. Also in the findings, it has shown that the live television viewing started to decrease as well.

The success of streaming services is also connected with the content they are making. Cook (2014) analyzed the success of Netflix by showing the statistics and the reactions for their original content. By making unique products which are different than the mainstream content, Cook believes that these companies improve their brand name and in result, more subscribers join. Similarly, Jenner (2015) analyzed streaming services' original content by binge-watching phenomenon. More successful shows according to the audience ratings and reviews are tend to be watched successively. That also shows the system of content, audience and the reception by the audience.

1.4 Methodology

This paper will analyze the evolution of television into the internet based streaming services. By looking to the history of television and the streaming platforms, further predictions will be made. In order to achieve the goal, articles and researches will be reviewed and analyzed with former media theories. Convergence and remediation theories upon the television will be the basis of the theoretical part of the research to understand the medium accurately. Combining that qualitative analysis with statistics, numbers gathered by the streaming companies; a quantitative analysis will be made to understand the status and the success of the streaming platforms.

By combining these two methods; predictions upon the medium of television will be made. To fill the gaps in the relatively new area in the media studies, theory and data analysis methods will be made in order to make a consistent research upon the topic.

The statistics will be used in this research paper will be coming from statistics companies like Statista and Nielsen. Furthermore, related statistics to the companies Netflix and Amazon will be used directly to show the size and the revenues of these companies; and in general, the industry itself in the face of traditional television industry.

2 Process of the Evolution

2.1 History of Television

There is no doubt that, television have altered our lives since the 1950s. In order to understand the evolution of the television; the steps of this evolution must be shown. Through some steps, television have evolved into a different form with the help of internet. Now, the television we know today is non-linear, consumer-driven and supported by other media elements like social media. The very process of the evolution of television has given us Netflix, Hulu and Amazon Prime. In order to analyze these video streaming services; first the history of television must be mentioned. First and foremost, invention of the television was not a single event. Invention of the medium, was actually merging of several other media elements like: electricity, telegraphy, photography and motion pictures, and radio. (Williams 1974, 14-15) Second half of the 19th century housed many technological breakthroughs and inventions. With combination of these breakthroughs, scientist have tried to find a way to transfer images to remote distances by combining principles of telegraphy.

Apart from these inventions, some scientists focused on this image transferring principle exclusively. In 1873, Irish scientist Joseph May have discovered the photoelectric effect using selenium bars. (Peters 2000, 3) That meant, by the help of sunlight; light intensity could be transmitted. 1875 George Carey in Boston, created a panel with bulbs and photoelectric cells jointly. By that, an image could be seen with the help of electricity. (ibid, 3) This system had its flaws as the panel needed to much wiring in order to see a proper image. Constantin Senlecq improved Carey's idea in 1881. By combining the cells, lamps and two rotating switches placed on the panels; Senlecq achieved to eliminate the wiring into a single wire. (ibid, 4) These were significant breakthroughs in the way transmitting image over electricity; yet the panels proposed for the idea were complicated and housed too many elements on board. In order to simplify the panel, Paul Nipkow came up with a different system in 1884. A beam of light was sent into a rotating disc containing small holes; Nipkow achieved to find a way to transmit image continuously for a small period of time. (ibid, 4) Yet once more, even the system has simplified; method was not suitable for large scales.

After these researches; improvements in physics have opened a new door to scientists. Electron have become the key element in the studies. In 1897, Karl Ferdinand Braun invented the cathode ray tube; which consisted of two electromagnets and a fluorescent screen. (ibid, 5) By the help of the electron beam, movement could be seen from the screen.

The cathode ray tube invented by Braun then modified by various scientists. In 1908, Campell Swinton came up with a system consisted of two cathode ray tubes both at the sending and receiving ends. (ibid, 5) That meant, the intensity of the electrons could be adjusted accordingly to the light intensity of the image. With the progression in the science and technology, selenium cells were replaced by potassium cells, then triodes respectively; which were faster to change the light intensity accordingly. (ibid, 7)

In 1925, Scottish engineer John Logie Baird, came up with a system that could show white letters on a black background. (ibid, 7) The image was produced by two discs in the system; so, it was not showing the real time. Yet, in 1926 Baird achieved to show a real scene of a person; with 30 lines and 5 frames per second. (ibid, 7) The attempt was seen as the first live television broadcast, and the machine Baird created was actually the first television. Baird called the invention as "televisor" (ibid, 10) The word "television" was not used for a long time to name devices that could transmit images. One of the first names given to the system was "télectroscope" or "electrical telescope". (ibid, 6) Then the German word "Fernsehen" was proposed by German scientist. (ibid, 6) Fernsehen means seeing the far in German which was explaining the purpose of the device. Later on, the French word télévision was used in 1900 by Constantin Perskyi; which was caught on and was used in many other languages to define the device (ibid, 6).

After the successful attempt by Baird, many scientists used the same principle to make their own television systems. In March 1935, German scientists have initiated a television service in Berlin; which would have broadcasted the Olympic Games in the 1936. (ibid, 11) People in Berlin and Leipzig could have seen the real time Olympic Games in particular viewing saloons which are called "Fernsehstuben". (ibid, 13) 1936 Olympic Games were the first biggest event which was televised to the public audience. As the technology spread around the world, new countries started television broadcasts and scientists continued working on the device to improve it.

In 1928, Baird achieved to make the first color demonstration in television. Later on, scientists like H. E. Ives, Georges Valensi and Peter Goldmark abled to improve Baird's color filters. (ibid, 17) By that the three colors green, blue and red could be seen separately on the screen. Following these researches in 1953, National Television Systems Committee (NTSC) was established to make a standard in the industry. (ibid, 17-18) Committee has structured a color television system that the user can adjust hue, saturation and the brightness. (ibid, 18) NTSC system was launched in 1954 in United States. (ibid, 18) Later on, the name for color television standard have become NTSC globally. Dr. Walter Bruch from Germany came up with a system called Phase Alternation by Line (PAL) in 1963. (ibid, 18) The principle Bruch have found was different from NTSC system, yet the outcome was the same. NTSC and PAL systems became available in England, Germany and France in 1967; with color broadcasting channels. (ibid, 18) By these initiatives, the era of color television has begun.

With improvements in both the hardware and broadcast part, the television has become an important medium for the 20th Century people. One of the most important events in the way of television history was the 1964 Tokyo Olympics. Japan broadcasted the games in High Definition quality. (Bayus 1993, 6) With investments in the industry, HDTV has become widespread all around the world starting from the 1980s. The HDTV movement in Europe started later than Japan. 1990 World Cup Italy and 1992 Barcelona Olympics were broadcasted in high definition by selected television channels. (ibid, 7) High definition broadcasting in United States has started after a government initiative in 1988, and has become prevalent in the following years. (ibid, 7) In parallel with the broadcasting, the hardware of the television has also been progressing. Plasma, LCD and LED televisions have been developed respectively since the 1960s. The quality of the broadcasting and also the viewing have been changed and developed radically since Baird invented the first television in 1920s and yet; the change continues even today.

2.2 Video-on-Demand - Netflix & Amazon Prime

Video-on-Demand services are the part of new media structure these days. Video-on-demand basically means a system that gives the consumer the liberty of choosing the content, watching time and place. There are some characteristics of these services which changes the linear television model: "Generally available functions are pausing, rewinding, fast-forwarding and recording programs so that they could be watched later. Formats of VoD include free VoD, subscription VoD, which requires an extra month fee usually for unlimited use of VoD services, and Pay-per-View VoD." (Kovacs 2015, 11) As could be seen, consumer is able to watch the content desired at any time with capabilities of interrupting or continuing and any time. Netflix and Amazon Prime are examples for subscription VoD; yet there is another sub-category for these services. Over-The-Top term is used to explain internet based platforms which require an internet connection usually by service providers. (ibid, 11) Though, Netflix and Amazon are independent companies which only fulfill the internet part of this category. Therefore, as a more general and accurate analysis, these services will be categorized as subscription based Video-on-Demand services or Video-on-Demand in this research. Video-on-Demand industry is expected to be worth around 61.5 billion dollars in 2019. (Rohan 2015) In this developing market Netflix and Amazon Prime are the biggest companies in subscribers and revenue.

Netflix was founded in 1997 by Marc Randolp in California, United States. (Kovacs, 2015, 20) Company first started as a DVD rental company then and in 1999, Netflix presented a subscription method for DVDs for a monthly-fee. (ibid, 20) With growing in the rental industry, company shifted to online streaming in 2007. (ibid, 20) Since 2007, Netflix have increased their revenues and market share and become the biggest company in the video-on-demand industry.

"Netflix is the world's leading Internet television network with over 93 million members in over 190 countries enjoying more than 125 million hours of TV shows and movies per day, including original series, documentaries and feature films. Members can watch as much as they want, anytime, anywhere, on nearly any Internet-connected screen. Members can play, pause and resume watching, all without commercials or commitments" (Netflix, 2017).

As of 2016, 94 million people have subscribed to Netflix's services, over 50 million from United States. (Statista, 2016, I) Therefore, 54% of United States households have Netflix access in 2017. (Statista, 2017, II) The percentage of that access was 28% in 2011. (ibid.) In just 10 years, Netflix has become the leader in the subscription based video market with an increasing rate. One of the important factors bringing this title is Netflix's original programming. Different than traditional television series productions, Netflix does not air pilots; makes an entire season available without any hesitation (Sharma 2013, 2). This strategy makes Netflix unique in original programming because no other company gamble without any feedbacks. "Everything that makes Netflix's programming distinctive-surrendering control to creators, releasing all episodes of a season at once, keeping its viewership data private rather than participate in the ratings game." (LaPorte 2014, 66) These uncommon strategies have earned Netflix millions of subscribers, Emmy awards for the programs. Due to these facts, Netflix was given the appellation of "It's not TV. It's Netflix." (ibid.) By drawing a unique audience using the internet subscription system, Netflix continues growing increasingly.

Amazon company was founded by Jeff Bezos in 1994, United States. (Schneider 2017) The company was an online bookstore at the beginning; then become an online shopping store selling variety of goods including electronics, clothing, music and movies. (ibid.) By expanding the product range, Amazon has become the biggest online store in the world. Amazon's net sale revenue in 2016 was 136 billion dollars. (Statista, 2016, III) In 2017, Amazon offers an employment opportunity for more than 270 thousand people worldwide. (ibid.) With different operation areas, large number of employees and being active in various companies Amazon has also entered the Video-on-Demand sector. Amazon Prime was launched in February 2005 as a shipping membership in the first instance. (Amazon, 2017) That included free shipping for a year and some deals from Amazon.com in return for one-year subscription. Aside from these deals and free of charge shipping, Amazon included music, movie and television series content streaming into the Prime system to increase the subscribers.

"Prime members enjoy fast, free unlimited shipping on more than 30 million items, as well as unlimited streaming of tens of thousands of movies and TV episodes, more than one million songs—and thousands of playlists and stations with Prime Music, early access to select Lightning Deals all year long, free secure, unlimited photo storage in Amazon Cloud Drive with Prime Photosone and one free pre-released book a month with Kindle First." (ibid.)

With existing shipping and store deals, Amazon included not only media streaming; but also cloud service access and some e-books for their device. By these additional promotions, Amazon Prime is an unorthodox Video-on-Demand service in the market. The revenue of retail subscription services inside the 136 billion dollars is 6.4 billion dollars in 2016. (Statista, 2016, IV) In 2014, subscription service revenues were 2.76 billion dollars. (ibid.) Amazon have not made the subscription number public yet; analyst Morgan Stanley have calculated the revenues of Amazon from the streaming department with the average subscription fee. The research shows that Amazon Prime has at least 65 million subscribers globally as of beginning of 2017. (Business Insider, 2017) Most of these subscribers joined beginning from 2014; in fact, Amazon states that in 2014 Prime subscribers were doubled globally. (Amazon, 2017) Just before that exact year Amazon executives held a meeting to discuss the growth plan of the subscription services. "Like Netflix and Hulu, the company has built an extensive library of TV and movies. But ultimately it determined that original programming was critical to attract and retain subscribers." (Sharma 2013, 2) By deciding to make their original programming, Amazon spared a budget of 1 billion dollars for the task in hand; by the way Netflix was investing 2.5 billion dollars at the time. (ibid.) Anyhow, by that initiative Amazon Prime gained significant subscribers and by that extension revenues started increasing gradually.

2.3 Convergence and Remediation

To understand the changes in the media in the 21st century, theorists have made some analysis and assumptions by looking to the cumulative data. Nowadays, new media term is widely used to define current media environment. New media consists of traditional media elements combined with internet or computer technologies and capabilities. By that, the medium in question combined with the new elements becomes a new one. Remediation term means improvement in English and it is widely used to define the new media. Jay David Bolter based his researched on new media upon the term remediation. Book defines the effect of new media on television medium as: "This is not like TV only better." (Bolter 1999, 3) This inference is the basis of remediation theory while analyzing technological developments and its' effects on media. With contribution of new agents, existing media changes; becomes a new one different from the previous state. Bolter perceives that these modifications are obligatory and positive for the existing medium:

"Like film, television need to remediate digital media in order to survive… Although traditional broadcast television faces a significant challenge, it may yet be able to merge or "converge" with computer-controlled media without losing its identity. In the meantime, producers of television are busy exploiting digital technology to enhance their medium's claim to immediacy." (ibid, 185)

As could be seen, Bolter purports that the change is inevitable, and the television industry must use the new elements in order to create better and more emerging content for their audiences. One of the different views in the Bolter's book belongs to Marshall McLuhan.

McLuhan puts the audience in the center when analyzing media and television in his time. According to McLuhan's technological determinism; if the technological changes effect the medium of television, it will not be television after all and would lose the characteristics and purpose by changing. (ibid, 187) Yet, it could be said that the new television would create its own audience and even if the message changes; there will be a new one created. This is the situation of today's media and television; video on demand services, internet, YouTube are supporting the television medium at the same time. Still, Bolter and McLuhan's implications are correcting that the television that we know have changed by this remediation process.

Another perspective in understanding of new media is convergence. Convergence means gathering in a certain point of several different elements. Henry Jenkins approached new media by analyzing the subject with the convergence method.

"By convergence, I mean the flow of content across multiple media platforms, the cooperation between multiple media industries, and the migratory behavior of media audiences who will go almost anywhere in search of the kinds of entertainment experiences they want. Convergence is a word that manages to describe technological, industrial, cultural, and social changes depending on who's speaking and what they think they are talking about." (Jenkins, 2006, 2-3)

Convergence could mean cooperation, mutualisation between industries; different media elements or different technologies. Yet, convergence and remediation might seem similar; these two elucidations are different. Remediation means change or a rearrangement but convergence is a gathering of different elements. Joao Canavilhas clearly defined the differences between these two theories by stating:

"While convergence implies a new language that integrates previous contents, remediation can be an accumulation of contents from different origins distributed in the same platform. In this sense, convergence is always remediation, but not all remediations can be considered convergences, because the latter implies integration and not mere accumulation of contents." (2012, 9)

Canavilhas asserting that the changes in the television medium are both should be explained by convergence and remediation. With internet, audience can select the watching pattern on their own by breaking the linearity concept of the television. (ibid, 14) That could be explained by remediation which is a change. Yet, online television and video-on-demand services are gatherings of television and internet in the same time and forming a different medium. Also new technologies like mobile devices and smartphones are also effecting media with capabilities of showing news, television series which is a different industry. (ibid, 17-18) These two separate theories will be the basis of this paper, remediation and convergence are the reasons and results of the changes in the media from traditional to new. Moreover, the changes in the television industry and media are obvious and rapid.

2.4 Effects of the Remediation and Convergence

In this part, effects of remediation and convergence by the digitization on television will be analyzed. Some of these outcomes have changing the core characteristics of television and creating new ones in the industry. Clearly, with Video-on-Demand services, internet and other forms of systems that streams content; television is losing the typical characteristic which is linearity. With traditional television, content and programs are in a flow which cannot be interrupted or changed. "Time shifting, video-on-demand and wider digitization undermine the very notion of continuity and flow." (Bulck, & Enli 2010, 13) The flow of the sequences of television could be adjusted, re-arranged or paused by the digitization and convergence of other technologies with television. A research was conducted in United States asking how people consume television content as of 2012. 23% of the contenders said they are watching more reruns of drama series rather than live watching, 25% said more about comedies, and 26% for movies aired on television. (Statista, 2012, V) Similar research was made by Nielsen in United States monitoring how people watched specific television series. Season 1 of Dexter series was watched with a rate of 69% live in 2006. In 2009, when the season 4 was on air; that rate decreased to 53%. Later on, Homeland season 1 live watched with a rate of 45%, then dropped to 32% in 2013 for the season 3. (Statista, 2014, VI) Technological changes which provides the opportunity to the audience that content could be watched anywhere and anytime. The live rating of the television series was decreasing because of the changes in the media and technology industries. William Urrichio explains the importance of liveness in television by:

"One of the oldest elements in television's definition was its potential for liveness. It defined television conceptually in the 19th century, distinguished it from film for much of 20th century, and although it has largely been supplanted by video in order to enhance the medium's economic efficiencies, liveness (even in the era of seven-second delay) nevertheless remains a much-touted capacity. Even slightly delayed, televised sports events, breaking news and special events attest to the medium's conceptual distinction from film, which was, for the duration of its photochemical history, emphatically not live." (2009, 31-32)

With the remediation and convergence mentioned, television started losing its edge, liveness and becoming like an another medium, cinema by video-on-demand services. Consumers are able to watch television content today like movies anytime in platforms like Netflix and Amazon Prime. One of the things changing by the dissolving of linearity and liveness is content. In Bulck & Enli's research about the liveness phenomenon, it has stated that public service broadcasters' wording about continuity and linearity should change as well. "… the key issue in 'liveness' might not be the live technological transmission, but the 'rhetorical" inclusiveness created when TV-presenters look directly into the camera and talk of 'now', 'today', 'here', and 'we'. The announcers serve a rhetoric function of insisting on the 'liveness' of the television broadcasting." (2010, 19) By changing the linearity of the medium and converging with other systems like streaming, television started losing the liveness feature. Plus, content like broadcasting, programs announcing and news reporting on television have to change similarly. Terms like "today", "here", "this morning" might not mean to a viewer who is watching the content online from a different place in a different time. Convergence of other systems have changed the television's consumption by the audience, especially with the streaming and on-demand services. Place and time has lost the meaning in television studies by the changes.

Liveness and linearity's dissolution in television created a similar new phenomenon as well. The audience's viewing habits have started to change. "Binge-watching" term has started to use to define television series marathons by watching entire seasons in a small period of time. Once again, this change contradicts with the traditional television and television series. In a research United States in 2016, people who have cancelled their cable or satellite televisions were surveyed. 18% of the people said that they cancelled their television service because they prefer binge-watching. (Statista, 2016, VII) Netflix for example, airs an entire season for a television series in a specific day. By that, consumers are able to watch multiple episodes successively without waiting like normal television. Yet, as stated, television series were not like that; people were expecting a final episode for an entire week without knowing what would happen. "This is interesting because traditionally, content has been designed for scheduled broadcasts, which has guided production to focus on fixed lengths (such as 25 minutes of content with 5 minutes for advertisements) If, indeed, viewers like binge watching, television shows could become longer, and there might be room for more creativity and personalization when most of the consumption is via on-demand streaming." (Mahanti 2014, 4-5) By removing the scheduled airing times and advertisements, people could watch more of content successively without interruptions. In United States, 2014, contenders to a research have answered the reasons to watch original series on the internet. 56%

said that they prefer watching on their own schedule, 38% answered they could skip commercials, 35% said they could watch multiple episodes and 33% said it houses less commercials. (Statista, 2014, VIII) That becomes a vicious circle for television channels to be watched because people would prefer longer shows without interruptions and without waiting times. Also, Mahanti states that this system could bring creativity to the television shows as well, by not arranging the programs to a schedule. Mareike Jenner proposes a similar approach with video-on-demand and binge-watching. "The VOD industry takes advantage of the autonomy and agency implied in binge-watching by using publication models and marketing (original) serialized drama over the content. But binge-watching is also a way to describe 'watching VOD', understanding it as decidedly different from 'watching TV'', one being autonomously scheduled and active the other programmed by broadcasting institutions, implying a potentially passive viewership. (2015, 14) So, the binge-watching is not a method of watched successive episodes of a series only; but at the same time shows the structural differences between traditional television and autonomous structure of video-on-demand services which are interactive.

Another big effect of convergence and remediation is people are watching less television compared to the past. The research by Nielsen shows that an average American adult watches 20 minutes less live television each day in 2014 compared to 2012. (The Total Audience Report, 2014, 10) Addition to that, the phenomenon of "cord-cutting" has become popular in the recent years. In 2010, 18.9 million households were not paying for a television service in United States and that number increased to 20.7 million in 2012. (Statista, 2016, IX) The projected number in 2021 is estimated around 33.3 million households; supporting that the phenomenon is rising. The reasons of cord-cutting are the price and the advantages of internet based streaming systems: " 'Whatever show you want, whenever you want, on whatever screen you want' [Lotz]. In other words, they demand a personalized television menu, pret-a-porter, and possibly for a good price deal." (Mazzoli 2015, 200)

As mentioned above, by changes in viewing habits; people tend to like and prefer video-on-demand services over cable/satellite systems. According to the cord-cutting research, the main motivation was that prices being too expensive by 80% in United States, 2016. Second motivation was using Netflix, Hulu or Amazon Prime by 48%. (Statista, 2016, VII) In Latin America, 2016 again, first reason was the prices; second one was not using it enough and the third was finding similar content online. (Statista, 2016, X) Again, competitive prices from streaming platforms have affected television subscriptions like satellite and cable; and also, television viewing is also decreasing with the rise of video-on-demand services. Another research shows young people's attitude towards traditional television. Average television viewing weekly for an American aged between 18-24 was 26.5 hours in 2011. In 2013, that number has dropped to 23.5 hours and 16.25 hours in 2016 respectively. (Statista, 2016, XI) So, traditional television viewing has been dropping, especially in the younger audience; compared to the rising streaming systems.

Another effect of the digitization on television is forming of new forms of content or programming by the changes. "It is true that media forms are merging, a to study them in isolation often overlooks not only the technological/industrial convergences but also the cultural convergences that take place among film, television, literature, music, and fine arts." (Spiegel 2005, 84) Separating the changes in the medium and the content would be a fallacious method while analyzing the television. "New kinds of entertainment and information programs and services will emerge where interaction is a central and necessary feature." (Lee & Lee 1995, 17) Once again, emerging systems and the content of the television should not be examined separately in media these days. For example, original programming by video-on-demand services were not so common couple of years before. In 2012, there were 3 original series aired online in the United States, which increased to 57 in 2016. (Statista, 2017, XII) Previously presented cord-cutting research in the United States have shown that 11% of the contenders cancelled because they are mostly interested in original series airing online. (Statista, 2016, VII) Once again, emerging elements have been forming in the television by the convergences and the audience prefer these compared to the traditional television content.

The most important source of financing for television is advertisements. Programs are being made by the advertising money and the industry is depending on the money from advertising. When looking at one of the biggest television industries in the world, United States, advertising revenue in 2004 was 47.2 billion and in 2013, the numbers has become 47.9 billion dollars. (Statista, 2013, XIII) So, there is no significant increase; in parallel with the television industry's growth. In the same time between 2011 and 2015; revenue from ad-supported mobile video content has tripled in the United States and have earned the share of 16.5 of the total mobile video market. (Statista, 2017, XIV) While the television advertising remains unchanged, ad-supported video advertising has been increasing. That was foreseen by some of the theorists who have been analyzing the convergence in the media. Barbara and Robert Lee have deduced that by the technological changes and interactive television's rise, advertisements and commercials on television have to change as well, by becoming more interactive. (Lee & Lee 1995, 17) By looking to the change in the advertising spending by medium, effect of the convergence could be seen. Mobile internet has increased by 47% and projected to grow 34% in 2016 and 2017 respectively. The increase in the internet spending is 14% and 13%, television spending is only 2.8% and 1% in the same period. (Statista, 2017, XV) In 2019, it is expected that the sum of mobile and desktop internet (will have the 26% and 15% share of the market respectively), will exceed the television advertising (33%) global spending. (Statista, 2017, XVI) As could be seen, the trends in the advertising has been changing.

"The disruption, which characterizes contemporary commercial television in the form of advertising, breaks and viewer-zapper activity will most likely be minimized by economic strategies more appropriate for a fragmented channel environment and by new selection mechanisms [the possibilities are many: product placement, pay-per-view, near video on demand]" (Urrichio, 2005, 255)

Television has been losing in the advertising market compared to the rise of internet and video services. With people watching less television or not watching it more increasingly like in the past, advertising revenues have started decreasing; which will be effecting traditional television crucially.

The convergence and remediation have not effected the traditional television medium positively. In this part, some of the effects on the medium has been covered. Yet, video-on-demand or video streaming platforms are effected positively by these changes because, these systems are results of these changes. Rise of subscription based internet Video-on-Demand platforms have been rising and ingathering consumers every day. As growing, with the investments; companies are expanding their databases and creating more original content. That potentially results as new consumers. With that growth rate and popularity, video-on-demand services are overcoming traditional television industry as of today; just like in other media channels where new overcomes traditional.

3 Success of Video-on-Demand Services

As exhibited in the previous section of the research, traditional television has been changing by the technological advancements, convergences with other media channels and industries. Internet based subscription Video-on-Demand services like Netflix and Amazon Prime on the other hand, are consequences of these changes in the media. End product of these convergences and new media system is overcoming the old states in entertainment. Subscription streaming has increased by 23% in 2016, whereas DVD / Blu-Ray sales decreased by 10%, and DVD / Blu-Ray subscriptions decreased by 17% in United States only. (Statista, 2017, XVII) Compared to traditional television, Video-on-Demand has been growing with an increasing rate and these services are affined with new media and the outcomes of it. By that, subscription numbers, content and the investments in the demand industry increases each year. In North America between 2014 and 2016, share of consumers who have subscribed to three or more streaming services increased from 9% to 19% respectively. (Statista, 2016, XVIII) As could be seen, these services are growing rapidly and becoming popular in the industry. In this part, the factors effecting the growth and the success of video-on-demand services will be analyzed.

3.1 Factors Effecting the Growth of Video-on-Demand Services

3.1.1 Prices of Video-on-Demand Services

Prices of the Video-on-Demand services are structured in order to compete with the traditional television, DVDs and Blu-Rays. With almost a same price of a movie ticket, a disc movie or television show; subscribers can watch unlimited material. Netflix is currently priced at $7.99, $9.99 and $11.99 for standard resolution, high-definition and 4K per month with 1 month free-trial respectively. The prices in different countries are determined similarly with the par of exchange and the economic status of the country in question. For example, in Turkey prices are t15,99, ₺27,99 and ₺39,99 respectively. (Netflix, 2017) Also in order of this pricing, users can watch content in 1, 2 or 4 screens at the same time. (ibid.) By that, consumers are able to use these plans with family members or friends. Amazon Prime is priced similarly to Netflix, $8.99 for video content, $10.99 for free-shipping, music streaming, e-book subscription and photo storage for per month. Annual pricing is $99 dollars and college students can have a discount with 6 months of free-trial and some special deals. (Amazon, 2017) These deals are very important for customers according to the statistics. In 2015, leading reasons to be an Amazon Prime member were free 2-day shopping (78%), video streaming (9%), promotions and other discounts (9%).

(Statista, 2016, XIX) This system by Amazon has become so successful that, the average Prime member spends \$2500 every year compared to Non-Prime members with an average of \$550. (Statista, 2016, XX) As shown by the consumer attitude, users love deals and they are tending to spend more for shopping on the Amazon site. With cheap prices compared to legal physical content services like Netflix and Amazon Prime are becoming more successful every year. "What makes Over-The-Top services interesting at the individual level is that these services provide customers with a cheap and alternative way of consuming content. Not to mention that the interactive platform, though which the service is provided, is superior compared to traditional television platforms and therefore it increases the value-added feature of the service." (Kovacs 2015, 27) From the consumers' perspective, video-on-demand services are reasonable by the many perks comes with the subscription and low prices. For the content makers, video-on-demand is also profitable. By paying large amounts of fees to producers for the ownership rights and additional profits time to time, video-on-demand services are preferred by the producers and content makers recently. (Doyle 2016, 637) Traditional television services are not paying that amount of ownership fees compared to video-on-demand. Because in subscription based video-on-demand there are no middle men and factors effecting the revenues, subscription fees could be directly used for big payments. Plus, producers tend to like it according to the researches.

3.1.2 Advertisements

Video-on-Demand services are offering an advertisement free interface as presented in the previous part of the research. Exemplary, Netflix gathers its revenue from subscriptions. "Revenue is purely generated through fees, since Netflix does not sell advertisement and therefore its content is ad-free." (Kovacs 2009, 20) However, some Video-on-

Demand services are gathering revenues from advertising. Also compared with the live television advertising, the ad-rates of Video-on-Demand are increasing. (Fontaine 2013, 117) In the previous part of the convergence, it is stated that advertising for the mobile and internet is increasing contrary to the stable rate of television advertising. That has an effect on television advertising as well. In order to compete with the Video-on-Demand, television channels are actually decreasing the advertisement amount to keep commercials effective. (Gonzales, 2015) Although this is good for the audience, television companies will be losing potential revenue by doing that. In United Kingdom, number of advertisements seen daily per individual have decreased from 47 to 45 between 2013 and 2015. (Statista, 2015, XXI) Video-on-Demand services with commercials are also different from television commercials as well. In a study in United States 2015, reactions against the commercials in streaming was analyzed. 30% said that they are doing something else on the device until the commercial is over, 26% said they are doing something else away from the device and 22% said that they are watching the commercials. (Statista, 2015, XXII) That means, 22% of the people are potentially watching it directly and third of the audience are not away from the commercial environment which is a kind of exposure to the commercials. Also, the rate of the audience who are watching the ads are higher in the younger audience. Generation Y (ages 13-35) at 24%, Generation X (36-49) at 20% and Boomers (50-64) at 17%. (Statista, 2015, XXIII) That means younger audience is exposing more of the commercials, which is positive for advertising companies and the Video-on-Demand services to attract younger audiences.

3.1.3 Age and Generation Difference

Age and generation difference has a significant effect in Video-on-Demand market just like other new media elements. In 2016, 93% and 94% of 16-24 years and 25-34 years old internet users have accessed internet in order to watch video content respectively. That rate among 35-44 years is 90%, in 45-54 years 87% and the rate of 54-64 is %81. (Statista, 2016, XXIV) Young people tend to watch more video content online compared to older ones. In the matter of streaming content, the result is similar. In United States as of 2015, Gen Y (13-35) have watched streaming content with an average of 3 days a week, Gen X (36-69) 2.2 and Boomers (50-64) 1.9 days. (Statista, 2015, XXV) Young adults and teenagers tend to use more of the new video technologies compared to older audience as predicted. Mobile access rate of Netflix between generations has a similar outcome. Half of the Gen Y accessed from a mobile device, Gen X's rate is at 36% and Boomers have accessed with a rate of 30%. (Statista, 2014, XXVI) Another way to state the generation difference in the media is to divide the audience into Millennials (18-34) and Non-Millennials. Globally as of 2015, rate of Non-Millennials watching traditional television is 32%, Millennials" rate is 13%. The rate of Millennials in Video-on-Demand is 20%, Non-Millennials at 9%. (Statista, 2015, XXVII) In another research in 2016 United States, statistical data shows that Cable and Satellite TV usage increase as the age increases; yet Netflix and Amazon Prime subscription rate is decreasing by age increase. (Statista, 2016, XXVIII) The access rate of Netflix in United States by generations showing that Generation X and Y are at 73%, where Boomers are at 67% and Retirees at 56%. (Statista, 2017, XXIX) The difference is more obvious at Amazon Prime users. In United States, usage of Amazon Prime in Generation Y is 71%, Generation X at 54%, Boomers at 34%, and Retirees at 31%. (Statista, 2016, XXX) As could be seen, globally and in case of the biggest market of United States; younger audience has involved in the success of Video-on-Demand services. Yet, the older generation's usage is also increasing but not same as the younger audience. Share of American adults who streamed Netflix daily in 2011 was 6, the number increased to 23 in 2017. (Statista, 2017, XXXI) As exhibited, the generation difference has a substantial effect on Video-on-Demand, but the gap has been gradually closing between the generations.

3.1.4 Consumer-Driven Structure & User Experience

One of the most important factors effecting the success of Video-on-Demand services is the control of the audience over the medium. "Spacey (Kevin) credits the streaming-video service for daring to let creative talent run the show without interference, and for empowering viewers as well. <Clearly, the success of the Netflix model… proved one thing: The audience want the control.>" (LaPorte 2014, 64) Kevin Spacey attributes the success of Video-on-Demand services to the power of audience and the control of it over the medium. To reach the audience more effectively, Video-on-Demand services are analyzing users' data and habits: "Services are becoming key ingredients. Among this glut of VoD content live channels will keep a central role of curator. But their ability to analyze viewers' habit to then recommend, deliver and invoice the right content on the right device, over the right network is vital." (Fontaine 2013, 117) Recommendation by interests and viewing habits are the key pieces in Video-on-Demand services. In 2015, a research was made worldwide. Contenders said that personalized television content and television services based on personal viewing habits (32%), ratings of previously viewed content (32%) and recommendation by habits, age, gender and zip code (31%) are vital when viewing relevant content. Only 22% said that they are interested in non-personal recommendations. (Statista, 2015, XXXII) Netflix alone is spending more than $300 million in order to improve user experience and the recommendation system. (Fontaine 2013, 117) And by that, in United States Netflix has become the number one in customer satisfaction among the streaming services. Participants said that Netflix is easy to watch on television (72%), easy to use on other devices (60%), has interesting original content (60%) and has a reliable service (58%). Amazon Prime has scored 54%, 49%, 36% and 48% respectively in these areas. (Statista, 2016, XXXIII) Once again it has shown that, the user experience and ease of use are important things in interactive platforms like Video-on-Demand services.

Another important effect of this consumer-driven structure is the phenomenon of user ratings. User ratings a key role in content making and future decisions about the content. For instance, Amazon Prime uses surveys to gather data about the audience's requests, looks at ratings and monitor watching behaviors in order to understand and create appropriate content for their consumers. (Sharma 2013, 3) Like Netflix, as could be seen, Amazon is putting the audience in the center of their system by giving them the power to affect the content. Another consequence of this rating system is on another medium and industry which is DVD and Blu-ray sales. According to the research, ratings on Netflix and IMDb actually effects the sales on Amazon online store. Content with higher ratings tend to sell more and for the content with lower ratings it is the opposite: "In this study, we have shown that the valence of user reviews from Netflix and IMDb had a significant impact on DVD sales on Amazon. That reviews from one website can be a primary source of influence on purchase behavior on other websites has a direct bearing on online vendors' marketing efforts." (Baugher & Ramos 2016, 158-159) That is a good example for the convergence has been taken place in media that a newer technology and medium actually effects the other one, from another industry; in this case physical video content by user ratings.

3.1.5 Digital Age

3.1.5.1 Internet Usage

Internet usage around the world is increasing day by day and more people have access to content online. In 2005, there were 1 billion internet users around the world and in 2015, number of users have increased to 3.2 billion. In 2016, there was 3.5 billion internet users all around the world. (Statista, 2016, XXXIV) Also as of November 2014, 53% of the internet users around the world were under 35 years and 74% of them were under

45. (Statista, 2014, XXXV) With that increase in internet usage, the video data streamed to televisions by internet have also escalated. In 2015, 6,4 petabytes of internet video were streamed to television, next year that number has become 9 petabytes. It is expected that in 2020, 23 petabytes of internet video will be streamed to television. (Statista, 2016, XXXVI) With the help of internet, consumers increasingly stream internet video to their smart televisions. For internet based Video-on-Demand platforms, usage of internet and internet video streams are vital because they provide their service via internet and internet connected televisions are one of the devices which content could be viewed.

3.1.5.2 Mobile Device Usage

Usage of smartphones have also increased in recent years and it is believed that the rise will continue. In 2014, 1.5 billion people were using smartphones globally, in 2016 it has become 2.1 billion. As of 2020, 2.87 billion people will be using smartphones according to the statistics. (Statista, 2016, XXXVII) Daily smartphone usage has increased as the sales as well. In United States, average smartphone usage daily has increased by 40 minutes and become 1 hours 33 minutes in 2014 compared to 2012. (The Total Audience Report, 2014, 10) By that increase, the global mobile video traffic has increased significantly as well. In 2011, 300 thousand terabytes of mobile video were streamed. 5 years later in 2016, mobile video stream monthly was projected to be 6 million terabytes. (Business Insider, 2013) Also, media consumption in television, computers, radio and print has dropped repeatedly between 2009 and 2013; but mobile consumption increased by 37%. (ibid.) That mobile consumption consists not only of smartphones but tablets as well. There were 660 million tablet users in 2013 in the world and in 2016, there was 1.12 billion users. (Statista, 2016, XXXVIII) Daily tablet usage in United States has increased from 20 minutes to 160 minutes from 2010 to 2014. (Statista, 2015, XXXIX) The usage of tablets has also effected the Netflix viewing habits as tablet viewing of the platform has increased in 2014. (Cook 2014, 19) Globally in 2015, 27% of the Netflix users have watched content by their smartphones and 10% of them were using tablets. (Statista, 2015, XL) In 2016, the usage of smartphones while watching Netflix has increased by 82%, which was the biggest increase within the different devices. (Perry, 2017) With various devices support, Netflix has achieved to attract more consumers into their subscription plans and mobile devices are the most important ones compared to other devices which has internet connection. That is the same case for the Amazon Prime as well.

3.1.5.3 Smart TVs & 4K

With changes in the television content, the television sets are also changing in today's world. Number of internet connected "Smart TVs" in 2010 were 115 million around the world. In 2016, 584 million internet connected televisions were being used by consumers. It is estimated that in 2018, 760 million internet connected televisions will be used. (Statista, 2017, XLI) Average global price of a Smart TV in 2011 was 2100$ and it is projected to decrease at 1200$ in 2017. (Statista, 2012, XLII) That means more of the consumers around the world can afford to have a connected television set. Another new technology in television platform is the appearance of 4K or UHD televisions, which offer more resolution than normal HDTVs. In 2013, 900 thousands of 4K televisions were being used and that increased to 48 million in 2016. (Statista, 2017, XLIII) By that increase, more of the audience could be able to watch 4K content from their televisions. That is important because Netflix and Amazon Prime are offering 4K resolution for some of their library. It could be deduced that with the Smart TV and 4K / U-HDTV sale increase, more people will be able to watch Video-on-Demand content directly from their televisions with a better quality than the 1080p High-

Resolution. Consequently, people with new television sets are potential customers for these platforms.

3.1.6 Popular Culture & Role of Social Media

Social media has a key importance while dealing with new media in general. Most of the current internet users own various social media accounts. As of September 2015, 93% of all internet users had at least one social media account globally and that rate in the age group of 16-34 was 95%. (Statista, 2016, XLIV) The social media ownership has risen significantly in the last decade. One of the biggest markets in Video-on-Demand, United States, had 24% social media users in 2008 and in 2017, it has become 81% of the whole population. (Statista, 2017, XLV) With the social media rise, entertainment concept has started to change as well, usually in the younger audience. Globally, 64% of the Millennials have stated that Internet and social media are the best sources for entertainment in 2013. That rate in Europe is 82%. (Statista, 2015, XLVI) Also among Millennials, usage of other devices while watching television has risen. 70% of the Millennials were using mobile devices and 55% were using laptops while watching television globally as of 1st quarter 2014. (Statista, 2015, XLVII) In other words, audience were using other media elements while watching television content. In another research among internet users, participants were asked to answer that they were doing while watching television. 32% answered they were looking information about the content they are watching, 15% were sharing opinion about the content online and 10% were interacting with the content online as of 4th quarter 2013. (Statista, 2015, XLVIII) So, almost half of the audience were actually engaging with the television online. Globally, a research was made to learn about the consumers' attitude towards brands on social media and internet in 2014. People between ages of 16-34 said that they like when brands give power to the consumers by 54%, they are following social media accounts of brands for deals and discounts by 50% and 48% said they feel connected when brands are involved with popular culture. For the ages between 35-54, the answers to these questions were 44%, 38% and 36%. (Statista, 2014, XLIX) Briefly, consumers like to get involved in the brands operation and they like when brands involve with the social media and popular culture, especially the younger audience.

Having said that, in order to understand that situation's effect on Video-on-Demand; certain social media accounts of Amazon Prime and Netflix should be examined. Netflix has 33.2 million likes on their Facebook page and company shares relevant content in parallel with their programming. (Facebook, 2017) Instagram account of Netflix has 3.4 million followers (Instagram, 2017) and 2.98 million for the Twitter account. (Twitter, 2017) Amazon Prime mostly uses more of the Amazon accounts in order to promote their video services. Anyways, social media accounts of Prime have significant followers as well. In Twitter 330 thousand (Twitter, 2017) and in Instagram 60 thousand people (Instagram, 2017) follows Amazon Prime Video accounts. Over 400 thousand users have liked the Prime Video page in Facebook (Facebook, 2017) and these numbers are increasing with every new content and subscription. As stated, social media and popular culture concepts are important for the audience and companies like Amazon and Netflix are using it accordingly to attract more subscribers.

3.1.7 Original Programming

While presenting the data about the consequences of convergence and remediation, it has stated that original programming by Video-on-Demand services has increased significantly over the years. Netflix and Amazon Prime have different strategies in making their own programs. Netflix does not use pilot episodes while making original content and according to the producers, it improves creativity and the structure of the stories; without interrupting the series by pilot episodes. (Sharma

2013, 4) Amazon on the other hand, combines pilot episode technique with audience's reception and feedbacks. Different pilot episodes in genres are made by Amazon and published in order to get feedback from the audience. Then customers watch and rate the episodes they like and Amazon continues making these contents according to the feedbacks. (Cook 2014, 16) By combining pilot system and ratings form the audience, Amazon makes its original content in a unique way. In order to see the effect of these different methods, Netflix and Amazon Prime's original content ratings must be examined. In June 2014, 20% of Netflix users were watching original content and in December 2016, that rate increased to 32% in United States. (Statista, 2016, L) In the same period, Amazon Prime's original content rating among the U.S. users have risen to 31% from 4%. (Statista, 2016, LI) With different methods, both companies increased the viewing rates for their original content. Original programming is a key element in attracting new audience to these platforms, and also retaining them in order to continue subscribing. (Sharma 2013, 2) Original programming is an important factor while analyzing the success of these platforms and in each year, the number of original programming increases; as the subscriber numbers increase.

3.1.8 New Markets for the Video-on-Demands Services

In order to grow, Video-on-Demand services have to increase their operations globally. With the success in North America, Netflix and Amazon Prime has been launched in many countries around the world. Netflix has become available in nearly 200 countries in January 2016, excluding China, North Korea, Syria and Crimea. (Statista, 2016, LII) Whereas, Amazon Prime is available in 242 countries around the world as of December 2016. (Business Insider, 2016) Growing outside of United States means more subscribers and more revenues eventually. Yet, in the case of Netflix, company has been losing money internationally between 2014 and 2nd quarter of 2016. (Statista Digital

Market Outlook, 2016, 11) That loss results from the investments to the new countries: "Before they can generate 1$, they have to spend money to have a service that people would sign up for. By the nature of the beast, you have to invest upfront." (Laughlin 2016, 22) With these investments, Video-on-Demand industry attracts potential subscribers in new territories. As an illustration, in Western Europe subscription Video-on-Demand services' revenue has increased by 103% in 2014 compared to 2013. In Eastern Europe, the growth was 47%. (Statista, 2017, LIII) It is predicted that, Video-on-Demand market in Europe will be growing with an average of 3.2% annually until 2025. (Fontaine 2013, 117) By that, subscription based Video-on-Demand services will be increasing their revenues and subscriber numbers accordingly to the investments they have made in advance. According to the statistics, in United Kingdom between 2012 and 2016, the share of digital content consumers' rate in Netflix usage has risen from 7% to 27%. (Statista, 2016, LIV) That means more people are adopting the platform every year.

In another study, China and Europe's annual growth rate (CAGR) and key performance indicator (KPI) values were examined along with the market share in the regions. In 2016, China Video-on-Demand market was $0.9 billion dollars and Europe's was $3.5 billion. (Statista Digital Market Outlook, 2016, 7) In 2021, it is expected that the markets in these regions will be $2.9 billion and $5.1 billion dollars respectively. (ibid.) In order to compare, United States market was $9.5 in 2016 and will be around $11.5. (ibid.) That means, Europe and China alone will be equal to 70% of the United States market. Also, user numbers of streaming services will increase in these countries accordingly. In 2020, United States user numbers will start to decrease but in Europe and China, it will increase every year. (ibid.) In 2021, Europe and China's user numbers are expected to be around 150 million; passing United States' 82 million. (ibid.) In fact, it is expected that China's and United States' user numbers to be equal in 2021. With that growth in new areas, Video-on-Demand services are expected to grow; in parallel with the investments that have been made.

3.2 The Future of Television

Under some headlines, factors which could affect the success of Video-on-Demand services are examined in the previous section of the paper. By the convergences and remediation, the television medium has been reshaping every day. The audience and the society are in the middle of this change. Production, distribution and reception are stages that the audience has a great effect. All of the factors presented in the previous section are results of the convergences and remediation because by the changes, the audience is getting stronger and Video-on-Demand services are using this positively compared to traditional television. That said, the previous theories about media and society could be used in the new media as well; especially in television. "It is well known that Harold Innis (1951, 2007), Marshall McLuhan (1992), Neil Postman (1982) and Joshua Meyrowitz (1990) already analyzed the role of media in the society, starting with the assumption that culture and society are influenced and formed by the respective leading media of a historical phase." (Krotz 2014, 141) Those theorists have studied on the "medium theory" which is highly relevant to the topic in question. The audience and the medium are constantly effected by one and other. By that, both the medium (television) and society (audience) are changing in parallel with the needs of the audience and the method used by the producers for the television. Today, with the Video-on-Demand services, the desires and needs of the audience have become the most important factor while making content, distributing it, and getting reception. That being said, with all the findings gathered, a prediction will be made accordingly about the future of the television medium in the next section.

3.2.1 Content

With the decrease continuing in traditional television viewership and the increase in Video-on-Demand, streaming or web-based video materials; it is likely that content to continue changing. "It is also important to ask where we are in the technology development, behavioral change and content development cycle. That is, new television technologies often lead to new forms of viewing behavior which, in turn, lead to new content." (Einav 2009, 128) As the convergence continues between different industries and systems, new forms of technology could emerge, existing mediums and elements might change accordingly as well. "Some new technologies have emerged, but many more are likely to enter the marketplace over the next decade. This suggests that we should be actively monitoring changes in behavior and thinking about creative new content that will serve the digital viewer." (ibid.) Briefly, by looking to the current data, it could be said that the audience will be in power of deciding which content to be created and distributed on television just like today. Also, original programs by demand services are likely to increase in linear television might come up with similar content in genre, length and quality.

3.2.2 Audience

Today's television industry has shaped around the audience by both giving them the power and considering their opinion while created and distributing content. "Consumers are exploring new choices such as time shifted viewing, online viewing and video over portable media and their growing expectation of control over content consumption is not likely to recede any time soon." (ibid.) Yet, giving audience so much power over the medium could bring some problems. Subscribers to the Video-on-Demand services are basically consumers and these services are outcomes of consumerism. Binge-watching term is actually a good example for this argument because fundamentally, binge-watchers are consuming multiple episode successively which are meant to be watched in a long period of time. With more audience following that behavior, companies have to make more and more content in order to make the audience pleased. In general, the power of the audience over the content and medium is likely to continue; which give choices to watch content unbounded to place and time.

3.2.3 Platform of Television

The primary element which has gone through the change most, could be the platform of television itself. Traditional television concept is becoming less popular and less people watch it every day. Nevertheless, that does not mean the traditional television is dead just now. In United States 2013, 70% of the people were using cable, 41% Netflix, 26% Satellite and 18% Amazon to watch television. (Statista, 2013, LV) Even the internet based demand platforms' usage increase each year, majority of the audience also watches non-connected linear television. It is true that the change is going fast but the complete transformation to internet television is not likely to happen just yet. However, with that rate of increase in streaming and decrease in the live television viewing, traditional television might eventually disappear from the living room of the audience. "Consumers are increasingly relying on services other than cable television for their content consumption. These ongoing changes can potentially consign cable television to the history books, at least in the form we've known them in the recent past." (Mahanti 2014, 6) It could be stated that the change in the television will be accelerating in the following years but it is not possible to say when traditional television will disappear.

4 Conclusion

As put together with statistics, researches and theories; convergence and remediation currently changes the traditional television. New technologies like Video-on-Demand have been rising, effects the traditional medium again. By changes and improvements in the technology and the industries, audience and the content have also changed; now these two elements have become complementary elements in the new media. Audience has the control over the content, the platform and over the future of the medium as well. Despite that power, because of the various content and series which are being made by companies like Netflix, audience has become a consumer; constantly consuming content and demanding new ones. As shown with statistical data and theories, Video-on-Demand phenomenon against the television is genuine. Factors which have created these demand systems are now the biggest obstacles in television's way. Audience has power more than ever, content could be viewed anywhere and anytime. Low prices of demand services are also making negative effects to the traditional television.

It is shown that in television industry, on-demand services fill the gap of the television gradually. Scarcely, this translocation does not happen rapidly. And thus, Video-on-Demand services are giving the traditional television a notice, an opportunity to change as well because with the new media and convergence, old has to change and adapt, in order to survive.

Acknowledgement

This research paper is a Bachelor Thesis which was written at Bilkent University within the scope of COMD 482 VCP II under the supervision of Andreas Treske and Lutz Peschke.

5 Bibliography

Amazon Prime. *Amazon.* Retrieved from https://www.amazon.com/p/feature/zh395rdnqt6b8ea. Accessed on Apr. 10, 2018.

Amazon Video. *Facebook.* Retrieved from http://tr-tr.facebook.com/AmazonVideo. Accessed on Apr. 10, 2018.

Amazon Video. *Instagram.* Retrieved from http://www.instagram.com/amazonvideo/. Accessed on Apr. 10, 2018.

Amazon Video. *Twitter.* Retrieved from http://twitter.com/amazonvideo. Accessed on Apr. 10, 2018.

Prime College Deals. (2017). *Amazon.* Retrieved from https://www.amazon.com/b?ie=UTF8&node=6944229011 Accessed on Apr. 10, 2018.

Baugher, Dan / Ramos, Chris (2016): The Relationship of Online Netflix User

Reviews to Days to Sale for New DVDs on Amazon, *Academy of Marketing Studies Journal, 20* (Special Issue), 149-161. http://asbbs.org/files/ASBBS2014/PDF/B/Baugher_Ramos(P68-80).pdf Accessed on Apr. 10, 2018.

Bolter, Jay David / Grusin, Richard (1999): *Remediation: Understanding New Media.* Massachusetts, MA: MIT Press.

Business Insider. (2016, December 15). *Amazon Prime Video's Global Expansion Will Have Deep Ramifications on the TV and Streaming Industries.* Retrieved from http://www.businessinsider.com/amazon-prime-video-global-expansion-tv-streaming-industries-2016-12 Accessed on Apr. 10, 2018.

Business Insider. (2017, February 15). *Morgan Stanley Puts Amazon Prime Subscribers at 65M.* Retrieved from www.businessinsider.com/morgan-stanley-puts-amazon-prime-subscribers-at-65m-2017-2 Accessed on Apr. 10, 2018.

Buss, Sebastian (2016, Oct): *Digital Media: Video-On-Demand, Digital Market Outlook Statista*. Retrieved from https://punzhupuzzles.files.wordpress.com/2016/10/epublishing_outlook_2 016.pdf_Accessed on Apr. 10, 2018.

Canavilhas, Joao (2012): *From Remediation to Convergence: Looking at the Portuguese Media*. Covilha: Universidade da Beira İnterior Portugal. Retrieved from https://www.researchgate.net/publication/260228470_From_remediation_to _convergence_looking_at_the_portuguese_media Accessed on Apr. 10, 2018.

Cook, Camila Isabel (2014): *Netflix: A Stepping Stone in the Evolution of Television*. St. Petersburg, FL: University of South Florida St. Petersburg

Journalism and Media Studies. Retrieved from http://dspace.nelson.usf.edu/xmlui/handle/10806/11681 Accessed on Apr. 10, 2018.

Doyle, Gillian (2016): Digitization and Changing Windowing Strategies in the Television   Industry: Negotiating New Windows on the World. *Television & New Media,*   17 (7), 629-645. doi: 10.1177/1527476416641194.

Edwards, Jim (2013, November 24): TV Is Dying, And Here Are the Stats That Prove It. *Business Insider*. Retrieved from www.businessinsider.com/cord-cutters-and-the-death-of-tv-2013-11 Accessed on Apr. 10, 2018.

Einav, Gali / Carey, John (2009): Is TV Dead? Consumer Behavior in the Digital TV Environment and Beyond. In *Television Goes Digital* (115-129). New York, NY: Springer Science + Business Media. Fontaine, Gilles (4th Q. 2013): Television 2025: Video as a Service. *Digiworld Economic Journal,* 92, 115-118. Retrieved from http://eds.a.ebscohost.com/eds/detail/detail?sid=ee063db9-9048-492f-a07e-7c3d8e04fae5%40sessionmgr4009&vid=0&hid=4211&bdata=JnNpdGU9ZW RzLWxpdmU%3d#AN=1441756&db=eoh Accessed on Apr. 10, 2018.

Gonzales, Dave (2015, December): Thanks to Netflix, TV Will Have Fewer Commercials. *Tech Trends: PC Magazine Digital Edition*. Retrieved from http://eds.b.ebscohost.com/eds/detail/detail?sid=562a63c9-5942-400b-9093-b91ee2709889%40sessionmgr102&vid=0&hid=122&bdata=JnNpdGU9ZWR zLWxpdmU%3d#AN=111110617&db=f6h Accessed on Apr. 10, 2018.

Jenkins, Henry (2006). *Convergence Culture: Where Old and New Media Collide.*, New   York & London, NY, LDN: New York University Press.

Jenner, Mareike (2015): *Binge-Watching: Video-on-Demand, Quality TV and
        Mainstreaming Fandom.* Cambridge, CBG: Anglia Ruskin University.
Retrieved from
http://journals.sagepub.com/doi/full/10.1177/1367877915606485 Accessed
on Apr. 10, 2018.

Kovacs, Gabor (2015, May): *An Analysis of Strategies by Netflix in the Television
Market.* Aarhus, AAR: Department of Business Administration Aarhus
University. Retrieved from http://pure.au.dk/portal-asb-
student/files/86448002/Thesis_GaborKovacs_201208049.pdf Accessed on
Apr. 10, 2018.

Krotz, Friedrich (2014): Mediatization As a Mover in Modernity: Social and

Cultural Change   in the Context of Media Change. In K. Lundby (Ed.),
Mediatization of   Communication (pp. 131-162). Berlin, BER: Walter de Gruyter
GmbH.

Laughlin, Lauren Silva (2016, March 28): What's Next for Netlix? *Fortune.*
Retrieved from http://fortune.com/2016/03/28/netflix-stock-performance/
Accessed on Apr. 10, 2018.

LaPorte, Nicole (2014): Netflix: The Red Menace. *FastCompany.com,
February.*Retrieved from
http://eds.b.ebscohost.com/eds/detail/detail?sid=7e9dcedf-a1e1-4dfd-8db7-
e81613a987ee%40sessionmgr120&vid=0&hid=122&bdata=JnNpdGU9ZWR
zLWxpdmU%3d#AN=93498493&db=f6h Accessed on Apr. 10, 2018.

Lee, Barbara / Lee, Robert (1995): How and Why People Watch TV:
Implications

for the Future of Interactive Television. *Journal of Advertising Research, November-
December. Retrieved from* http://www.worldcat.org/title/how-and-why-people-
watch-tv-implications-for-the-future-of-interactive-television/oclc/757614227
Accessed on Apr. 10, 2018.

Lundgren, Lars (2015, January 6): The Forerunners of a New Era. *Media
History, 21(2),* 178-191. DOI: 10.1080/13688804.2014.991385 Retrieved from
http://www.tandfonline.com/doi/full/10.1080/13688804.2014.991385
Accessed on Apr. 10, 2018.

Mahanti, Anirban (2014). The Evolving Streaming Media Landscape. *IEEE
Internet Computing, January-February.* Retrieved from

https://ieeexplore.ieee.org/abstract/document/6756791/ Accessed on Apr. 10, 2018.

Mazzoli, Eleonora Maria (2015): Post-TV: Piracy, Cord-Cutting, and the Future of Television.   [Review of the book *Post-TV: Piracy, Cord-Cutting, and the Future of Television*, by Michael Strangelove] *Cinej Cinema Journal, 5.1*. Doi: 10.5195/cinej.2015.136. Retrieved from http://cinej.pitt.edu/ojs/index.php/cinej/article/view/136 Accessed on Apr. 10, 2018.

Netflix. *Facebook*. Retrieved from (http://tr-tr.facebook.com/netflix/) Accessed on Apr. 10, 2018.

Netflix. *Instagram*. Retrieved from (http://www.instagram.com/netflix/) Accessed on Apr. 10, 2018.

Netflix. *Twitter*. Retrieved from (http://twitter.com/netflix) Accessed on Apr. 10, 2018.

Overview. (2017). *Netflix*. Retrieved from https://ir.netflix.com/ Accessed on Apr. 10, 2018.

Perry, Monique (2017, February, 15): Small Screens Driving Audience Growth to Netflix. *Nielsen Report Media and Entertainment*. Retrieved from http://www.nielsen.com/au/en/insights/news/2017/small-screens-driving-audience-growth-to-netflix.html Accessed on Apr. 10, 2018.

Peters, Jean-Jacques (2000, February, 6): DVB - A History of Television. Retrieved from http://arantxa.ii.uam.es/~jms/tvd/tv_history.pdf

Prices. (2017). *Netflix*. Retrieved from https://www.netflix.com/tr/#this-is-netflix

Prime College Deals. (2017). *Amazon*. Retrieved from https://www.amazon.com/b?ie=UTF8&node=6944229011 Accessed on Apr. 10, 2018.

Rohan, Salgarkar (2015, February): Video on Demand (VOD) Market worth $61.40 Billion by 2019. *MarketsandMarkets*. Retrieved from http://www.marketsandmarkets.com/PressReleases/audio-video-on-demand-avod.asp Accessed on Apr. 10, 2018.

Schneider, Laura (2017, March 20): Overview of Amazon.com's History and Workplace Culture. *The Balance*. Retrieved from

https://www.thebalance.com/amazon-com-company-research-2071316
Accessed on Apr. 10, 2018.

Sharma, Amol (2013, November 1): Amazon Mines Its Data Trove to Bet on TV's Next Hit. *Wall Street Journal.* Retrieved from https://www.wsj.com/articles/SB1000142405270230420080845791638616378 39706 Accessed on Apr. 10, 2018.

Spiegel, Lynn (2005, Autumn): TV's Next Season? *Cinema Journal, 45, (1)*, 83-90. Retrieved from https://static1.squarespace.com/static/5101f04fe4b0527bec6f8a55/t/51a7704 6e4b061864c3b19f4/1369927750768/SpigelLynn_TV%27sNextSeason.pdf Accessed on Apr. 10, 2018.

Turrill, Dounia (2014, December): The Total Audience Report. *Nielsen.* Retrieved from http://s1.q4cdn.com/199638165/files/doc_presentations/2014/The-Total-Audience-Report.pdf Accessed on Apr. 10, 2018.

Urricchio, William (2005): *Television's Next Generation: Technology / Interface*

Culture / Flow In, Television After TV: Essays on a Medium in Transition. L. Spiegel, & J. Olsson (Ed.). Durham, NC: Duke University Press. Retrieved from http://web.mit.edu/uricchio/Public/pdfs/pdfs/flow%20edited.pdf Accessed on Apr. 10, 2018.

Uricchio, William (2009): The Future of a Medium Once Known as Television.

P. Snikkars, & P. Vonderau (Ed.): *The You Tube Reader (24-39)* London, LDN: Wallflower Press. Retrieved from http://web.mit.edu/uricchio/Public/pdfs/pdfs/Future%20of%20a%20Media .pdf_Accessed on Apr. 10, 2018.

Van den Bulck / Enli, Gunn Sara (2010): *Bye Bye 'Hello Ladies'? Announcers as Continuity   Technique in a Post-Linear Television Landscape.* London: Universieit Antwerpen & University of Oslo. Retrieved from http://citeseerx.ist.psu.edu/viewdoc/download?doi=10.1.1.664.6129&rep=re p1&type=pdf_Accessed on Apr. 10, 2018.

Williams, Raymond (1974): *Television: Technology and Cultural Form.* New York, NY: Shocken Books. Retrieved from http://stuartgeiger.com/williams-television.pdf_Accessed on Apr. 10, 2018.

6) References

I.   Netflix. (2017, January 19). Netflix Continues to Build Its Global Audience. *Statista*. Retrieved from https://www.statista.com/chart/7677/netflix-subscriber-growth/

II.   Leitchtman Research Group, MarketingCharts. (2017). Share of TV households with a Netflix subscription in the United States in 2011 and 2017. *Statista*. Retrieved from https://www.statista.com/statistics/686268/share-households-netflix/

III.   Amazon. (2017). Net sales revenue of Amazon from 2004 to 2016 (in billion U.S. dollars). *Statista*. Retrieved from https://www.statista.com/statistics/266282/annual-net-revenue-of-amazoncom/

IV.   Amazon. (2017). Global net revenue of Amazon.com from 2014 to 2016, by segment (in billion dollars). *Statista*. Retrieved from https://www.statista.com/statistics/672747/amazons-consolidated-net-revenue-by-segment/

V.   GfK. (2012, June). Effect of monthly Netflix use on regular TV consumption in the United States as of June 2012. *Statista*. Retrieved from https://www.statista.com/statistics/258823/effect-of-netflix-use-on-tv-consumption-in-the-us/

VI.   Showtime, Nielsen, Rentrak. (2014, July 23). How TV Watching Has Evolved Over the Past 8 Years. *Statista*. Retrieved from https://www.statista.com/chart/2484/tv-watching-habits/

VII.   TiVo, Digitalsmiths, VideoInk. (2016). What factors influenced your decision to cut off your cable/satellite service? *Statista*. Retrieved from https://www.statista.com/statistics/305416/cord-cutting-reasons/

VIII. MediaPost, comScore. (2014, October). Leading reasons for watching original TV programming on the internet in the United States as of October 2014. *Statista*. Retrieved from https://www.statista.com/statistics/333960/reasons-watching-tv-online/

IX.   Digital TV Research. (2010-2012). Number of households not paying for TV services in North America in 2010 and 2021 (in millions). *Statista*. Retrieved from https://www.statista.com/statistics/482958/number-cord-cutting-tv-households-north-america/

X.   Business Bureau, Rapid TV News. (2016, July). Reasons for cord cutting in Latin America in 2016. *Statista*. Retrieved from https://www.statista.com/statistics/689226/latam-cord-cutting-reasons/

XI.   Nielsen. (2015, July 3). Young Americans Turn Their Backs on Traditional TV. *Statista*. Retrieved from https://www.statista.com/chart/3613/tv-usage-by-american-teens/

XII.   HIS Markit. (2016, October 18). Online Platforms Double Down on TV Programming. *Statista*. Retrieved from https://www.statista.com/chart/6290/netflix-amazon-content-investment/

XIII.   Kantar Media. (2013). Broadcast TV advertising revenue in the United States from 2004 to 2013 (in billion U.S. dollars). *Statista*. Retrieved from https://www.statista.com/statistics/183366/ad-revenue-in-us-broadcast-television-since-2004/

XIV.   eMarketer. (2015). Ad-supported share of total mobile video content revenue in the U.S. from 2011 to 2015. *Statista*. Retrieved from https://www.statista.com/statistics/220621/ad-supported-share-of-us-mobile-video-revenue/

XV.   WARC. (2017). Year-over-year change of advertising spending in 2016 and 2017, by medium. *Statista*. Retrieved from https://www.statista.com/statistics/240679/global-advertising-spending-growth-by-medium/

XVI.   ZenithOptimedia. (2016, December). Distribution of global advertising expenditure in 2019, by media. *Statista*. Retrieved from https://www.statista.com/statistics/269333/distribution-of-global-advertising-expenditure/

XVII.   The Digital Entertainment Group. (2017, January, 18). Netflix & Co. Surpass DVD & Blu-ray Sales. *Statista*. Retrieved from https://www.statista.com/chart/7654/home-entertainment-spending-in-the-us/

XVIII.   451 Research. (2016, December). Share of consumers who subscribe to three or more streaming services in the North America from December 2014 to December 2016. *Statista*. Retrieved from https://www.statista.com/statistics/691518/multi-service-streaming-subscribers/

XIX.   eMarketer, RBC Capital Markets. (2015). Most popular reasons for users in the United States to join Amazon Prime from 2013 to 2015. *Statista*. Retrieved from https://www.statista.com/statistics/304945/us-amazon-prime-usage-reason/

XX.   Morgan Stanley Research, AlphaWise. (2016, October 12). Why Amazon Gives so Many Perks to Prime Members. *Statista*. Retrieved from https://www.statista.com/chart/6204/amazon-prime-members/

XXI.   BARB, Thinkbox. (2015). Number of television advertisements seen daily per individual in the United Kingdom (UK) from 2008 to 2015. *Statista*. Retrieved from https://www.statista.com/statistics/275546/number-of-tv-ads-seen-daily-in-the-united-kingdom-uk/

XXII.   GfK. (2015, May). Reactions to commercials during streaming of TV programs in the United States as of May 2015. *Statista*. Retrieved from https://www.statista.com/statistics/496091/usa-reaction-to-commercials-during-streaming-tv-programs/

XXIII.   GfK. (2015, May). Reactions to commercials during streaming of TV programs in the United States as of May 2015, by age group. *Statista*. Retrieved from https://www.statista.com/statistics/496122/usa-reaction-to-commercials-during-streaming-tv-programs-age/

XXIV.   GlobalWebIndex. (2016, 1st Quarter). Online video viewing penetration among internet users worldwide as of 1st quarter 2016, by age group. *Statista*. Retrieved from https://www.statista.com/statistics/272935/share-of-consumers-who-watch-online-video-by-age/

XXV.   GfK. (2015, May). About how many days a week do you watch streaming content on a TV set at home? *Statista*. Retrieved from https://www.statista.com/statistics/496063/usa-svod-to-tv-streaming-usage-weekly/

XXVI.   comScore, Digital Strategy Consulting. (2014, August). Share of Netflix viewers who consumed Netflix content from a mobile device in the United States in August 2014, by age group. *Statista*. Retrieved from https://www.statista.com/statistics/500020/mobile-netflix-viewer-share-age-usa/

XXVII.   L.E.K. (2015). Distribution of time spent with media among Millennials worldwide in 2015, by medium and age. *Statista*. Retrieved from https://www.statista.com/statistics/648620/millennials-time-spent-media-age/

XXVIII.   Statistic Brain Research Institute, US Census Bureau, Harris Interactive, International Strategy & Investment. (2016, January). Share of consumers who subscribe to selected pay TV services in the United States as of January 2016, by age. *Statista*. Retrieved from https://www.statista.com/statistics/680661/pay-tv-services-subscription-by-age/

XXIX.   Vantiv, Socratic Technologies. (2017, February). Share of consumers with an active Netflix subscription in the United States as of February 2017, by age group. *Statista*. Retrieved from https://www.statista.com/statistics/698020/netflix-subscription-by-age/

XXX.   Vantiv, Socratic Technologies. (2016, August). Share of online consumers in the United States who are Amazon Prime members as of August 2016, by generation. *Statista*. Retrieved from https://www.statista.com/statistics/609991/amazon-prime-reach-usa-generation/

XXXI.   Leichtman Research Group. (2017). Share of adults who stream Netflix daily in the United States in 2011 and 2017. *Statista*. Retrieved from https://www.statista.com/statistics/258922/average-netflix-content-consumption-in-the-us/

XXXII.   Ericsson. (2015). Interest in recommendation features for content and TV services worldwide in 2015. *Statista*. Retrieved from https://www.statista.com/statistics/468693/interest-recommendation-services-tv/

XXXIII.   Forrester. (2016, February 2). Netflix Beats Competition in Customer Satisfaction. *Statista*. Retrieved from https://www.statista.com/chart/7893/customer-satisfaction-video-streaming-services/

XXXIV.   Statista. (2016, July). Number of internet users worldwide from 2005 to 2016 (in millions). *Statista*. Retrieved from https://www.statista.com/statistics/273018/number-of-internet-users-worldwide/

XXXV.   comScore. (2014, November). Internet use by age group worldwide as of November 2014. *Statista*. Retrieved from https://www.statista.com/statistics/272365/age-distribution-of-internet-users-worldwide/

XXXVI.   Cisco Systems. (2015). Data volume of global internet video to TV traffic from 2015 to 2020 (in petabytes per month). *Statista*. Retrieved from https://www.statista.com/statistics/267222/global-data-volume-of-internet-video-to-tv-traffic/

XXXVII.   eMarketer. (2015). Number of smartphone users worldwide from 2014 to 2020 (in billions). *Statista*. Retrieved from https://www.statista.com/statistics/330695/number-of-smartphone-users-worldwide/

XXXVIII.   eMarketer. (2016, April). Number of tablet users worldwide from 2013 to 2020 (in billions). *Statista*. Retrieved from https://www.statista.com/statistics/377977/tablet-users-worldwide-forecast/

XXXIX.   eMarketer. (2014, June). Average daily media use in the United States from 2010 to 2014 (in minutes). *Statista*. Retrieved from https://www.statista.com/statistics/270781/average-daily-media-use-in-the-us/

XL.   Adweek, Netflix. (2015). Primary devices used for Netflix accounts during first six months worldwide in 2015. *Statista*. Retrieved from

XLI.   Digital TV Research. (2013, October). Number of connected TV sets worldwide from 2010 to 2018 (in millions). *Statista*. Retrieved from https://www.statista.com/statistics/247160/forecast-of-the-number-of-connected-tv-sets-worldwide/

XLII.   Frost & Sullivan. (2012). Forecast average selling price smart TVs worldwide from 2011 to 2017 (in U.S. dollars). *Statista*. Retrieved from https://www.statista.com/statistics/314631/smart-tv-average-selling-price-worldwide-forecast/

XLIII.   Consumer Technology Association. (2014). 4K Ultra HD TV unit shipments worldwide from 2013 to 2016 (in millions). *Statista*. Retrieved from https://www.statista.com/statistics/422402/4k-ultra-hd-tv-shipments-worldwide/

XLIV.   GlobalWebIndex. (2015, 3rd Quarter). Share of internet users worldwide who have at least one social media account as of 3rd quarter 2015, by age group. *Statista*. Retrieved from https://www.statista.com/statistics/499831/online-adults-with-social-media-account-by-age-worldwide/

XLV.   Edison Research, Triton Digital. (2017, March). Percentage of U.S. population with a social media profile from 2008 to 2017. *Statista*. Retrieved from https://www.statista.com/statistics/273476/percentage-of-us-population-with-a-social-network-profile/

XLVI.   Telefonica, Financial Times. (2013, February). Millennials: Best sources for entertainment in 2013, by region. *Statista*. Retrieved from https://www.statista.com/statistics/270958/best-source-for-entertainment-among-millenials/

XLVII.   GlobalWebIndex, We Are Social. (2014, 1st Quarter). Second-screening devices used by Millennials worldwide as of 1st quarter 2014. *Statista*. Retrieved from https://www.statista.com/statistics/307094/millennials-second-screen-devices-used-worldwide/

XLVIII.   GlobalWebIndex. (2013, 4th Quarter). The last time you were watching TV and using the internet, which of the following did you do? *Statista*. Retrieved from https://www.statista.com/statistics/295016/teens-tv-internet-second-screen-usage/

XLIX.   Havas Media. (2014, September). Consumers' relationship with brands worldwide as of September 2014, by age. *Statista*. Retrieved from https://www.statista.com/statistics/294844/consumers-age-relationship-brands/

L.   451 Research, Rapid TV News. (2016, December). Share of Netflix customers who watch original content most often in the United States from 2014 to 2016. *Statista*. Retrieved from https://www.statista.com/statistics/688978/netflix-original-content-viewership/

LI.   451 Research, Rapid TV News. (2016, December). Share of Amazon Video customers who watch original content most often in the United States from 2014 to 2016. *Statista*. Retrieved from https://www.statista.com/statistics/689014/amazon-video-original-content-viewership/

LII.   Netflix. (2016, January 7). Netflix's Global Expansion. *Statista*. Retrieved from https://www.statista.com/chart/4205/netflixs-global-expansion/

LIII.   Strategy Analytics. (2014). Change in over-the-top video revenue in Europe in 2014, by region. *Statista*. Retrieved from https://www.statista.com/statistics/330115/ott-video-revenue-growth-europe/

LIV.   Kantar Media, Ofcom. (2016). Use of Netflix to consume or share digital content in the United Kingdom (UK) from 2012 to 2016. *Statista*. Retrieved from https://www.statista.com/statistics/291467/use-of-netflix-to-consume-or-share-digital-content-in-the-united-kingdom/

LV.   PricewaterhouseCoopers. (2013, June). Cable Still Has the Edge Over Netflix in the U.S. *Statista*. Retrieved from https://www.statista.com/chart/1514/adoption-of-pay-tv-services-in-the-us/

Music-on-demand Trend
and Changing Music Consumer Habits:
How Do We Listen to Music Now?

Bora Yağız Sipahi[*]

Abstract

Do people have 'listening habits'? Are they changing now? Nearly 30 years ago, people could experience music only live or listen to it from radio and vinyl. Then the cassette format came out with Walkman. Afterwards, it was CD's and CD players' age. At the beginning of 00's music piracy and .mp3 format has exploded. Big technology companies have seized on it and created MP3 players. The last ring on the chain is music-on-demand services such as Spotify, Apple Music, Tidal, etc. in our age. This paper will analyze how music consumers' habits while listening to music are changing and how streaming services are affecting it with qualitative and quantitative research method. The research will focus on how users of these streaming services from different age groups used to listen to music (i.e Were they listening to an entire album? How they were listening to music before streaming services?) and how are they listening to music now (i.e How many times are they repeating over one song? Are they listening to albums entirely or are they listening to curated playlists?) And finally, what these streaming services are doing to change listener habits?

---

[*] Bora Sipahi, Bilkent University, Department of Communication and Design. Ankara/Turkey

Introduction

In many cases technological advancements made peoples' lives much easier and the world is getting integrated to technology in different areas of their livings day by day. Music is not an exception. Music has also changed entirely with new technologies. Composing music, producing music, distributing music became very different in the last 20 years. The changes that came to consuming part of music however made the biggest impact to music industry. Launch of Napster spread (and made it unpreventable) illegal downloads all across the world. The process caused serious decreases in profits of music market for a while as "music album sales have been decreasing over the last 15 years. In United States between 1999 and 2015, physical album shipments have decreased from 938 million to only 123 million. The decrease trend is worse for the music singles. In United States between 1999 and 2015, shipments of physical music singles have decreased from 75 million to 0.9 million units. (Gürmeriç 2016, 8)" Hence, illegal downloading era pushed not only record labels and artists but also entrepreneurs to seeking new ways of making money through music. Basically, artists needed money to keep on making music and record labels needed money to distribute music. However, music consumers needed to get convinced to pay for music, something that they can already reach without paying money, at first so that the music market can function again. In order to convince people, music-on-demand services offered consumers millions of songs. They offered algorithm-based, time-of-day based or mood-based playlists. They offered a social network-like environment where people can even follow their friends just like Facebook and Twitter. They offered increased sound quality when it is compared to .mp3 format. Smartphones became music players and music became mobile and accessible anytime and anywhere people want. The competition among these services paved the way to several innovations on how we experience music. Music market was unable to find an answer to the question of how to make people pay for music again for several years and the answer is provided by music-on-demand services. Launch of the music-on-demand services helped the re-functioning of music market and made the market profitable again for all the parties of it.

This paper will show how these services changed our experiences on listening to music. What changes they brought to our habits? Listening to music you like used to be something that needed effort in the past. A consumer needed to purchase albums or mixtapes physically, they needed to hear it on somewhere and chase it, they needed to wait for hours for it to be played on the radio. Even illegal downloading needed an effort. Fortunately, it all became much simpler. But how this simplicity affected our experience overall? This paper will reflect on how did we perceive music in the past and how do we perceive it now. The paper will explain the changes that music industry and music consuming got through, and the innovations of these services in order to gain profits chronologically. In order to display how did these changes affected consumer behavior, the results of a brand-new research will be discussed around the main concern of the paper: How does this new music listener profile explore and consume music in our age?

Theoretical Part

Technology changed the way people listen to and perceive music just like it changed everything in our everyday lives. In the past, the only way we can listen to music was radio and vinyl. Radio was (and actually still is) important for delivering people both old and new music and chance to expand their music taste. "Radio, with the introduction of features such as DJs, formats and listener requests, has a long history of experimenting with varying degrees of curation, listener agency, and control." (Morris/Powers 2015, 2) Peoples' love for music brought the need of mobile music devices. Although the cassette format came out in the 60's as a device of private recording and copying, it became popular in the 70's and 80's among music market as the portable cassette players' prominence. These devices offered a more convenient way of listening to music to people. The albums distributed mainly in cassette format until 90's when Compact Disks and Compact Disk Players took over cassettes' and portable cassette players' places in the 90's. CD format offered people to copy and store the audio files on computers easily when it is compared to cassette format, which in some form paved the way of .mp3 format, music piracy and illegal downloading. This can be counted as the first hit that happened to the music industry as MP3 players have derived as a product which gives people the possibility of storing huge amounts of audio files in small (much smaller than CD players and Walkmans) portable devices. People forsaken paying for music with the beginning of 00's and headed for illegal downloading which was irrepressible for music labels and artists.

In early 2007, Apple launched its revolutionary smartphone model iPhone. Since then, mobile phones gained strong Internet abilities which turned them into small computers. This process caused the decline of MP3 players as nearly every smartphone that has been released after iPhone has music player feature in it. Now we entered the "post-download era" which is a term named by tech analysts seen as "the third destructive wave for the music industry in the last decade and a half" (Morris / Powers 2015, 2) with music-on-demand streaming systems such as Spotify and Apple Music. "These services turned smartphones into MP3 players with millions of tracks and can be used at almost any time and anywhere. (Zhang et al. 2013, 4)

This new environment brought by music-on-demand services is beneficial for all of its parties in economical aspect as average consumer paying 10 dollars per month for getting access to more than 30 million songs (or free in Spotify's Freemium case) and leave the negotiation phase to record labels and streaming services instead of paying 19 dollars per album while paying both record labels and artists at the same time, artists and music labels get paid to provide the content for streaming services' music library that is much more better than getting robbed with illegal downloading and streaming services increasing their revenues day by day.

Firstly, the peer-to-peer system needs to be examined in order to clarify this papers' quintessence. Music-on-demand services "relies on true streaming that means no copy of the original files ever resides on the user's computer, making one's library entirely dependent on a subscription to the service and/or a connection to the Internet. Although users may not encounter this as a limitation, it transforms recorded music from a durable and copiable good into 'single-use products (streams) that perish as they are consumed" (Anderson 2011, 160). With this trend, people gave up their habit of owning the music as "the latest surveys and researches show that the trend for buying traditional music products are decreasing in an increasing way. A statistic on the matter by Statista in 2016 pointed out: Audio Streams have increased at a point of 97%, CD Album Sales decreased by 12% between 2013 and 2016 in the United States. Digital Album Sales and Digital Track Sales decreased 18% and 24% respectively in that period" (Gürmeriç, 2016, 6) and began listening to music from cloud-like structures. "While this may seem a convenient way to manage a music library or to quickly obtain taste preferences, this practice also speaks to various ways in which even the music we own is becoming less and less ours" (Morris & Powers, 2015, 13). This is the result of huge amount of audio files that have been offered to subscribers which is nearly impossible to store in one computer or storage device.

Peer-to-peer system allows service providers to own and examine the user data for their own benefits. Which device is getting used (mobile or desktop), when the service is getting used (morning or late night), where the song is getting played (artist page, album page, playlist page), song skipping and stopping, likes or favorites, playlist types (mood-based, time-of-day based, genre-based) are some kinds of data that are available to the supplier. Hence, while competing, these services underlines their ability of music curation and recommendation. Spotify offers services such as algorithm-based radios, more social environment where you can follow your friends, favorite artists, music critics and their curated playlists respectively while Apple Music relies heavily on their human-curated playlists and algorithm database that offers personalized precise recommendations which are the primary vision of Beats Music (company that has been acquired by Apple and turned into Apple Music in 2015) as they aimed to solve the problem of 'what song comes next'. This brings us to the main question of this paper: Are music-on-demand services affecting our listening habits? And if so, how?

This paper's main concern is the change in the user behavior of music-on-demand subscribers. In the research part, the focus will be on how subscribers of these services from different age groups used to listen to music (i.e Were they listening to an entire album? How they were listening to music before streaming services? How do they discovering new music back then?) and how are they listening to music now (i.e How many times are they repeating over one song? Are they listening to albums entirely or are they listening to curated playlists? How do they discover music now?). Are they changing with the music-on-demand trend? Since music-on-demand is a new field in new media as market leader Spotify launched in 2007 and there aren't many updated pieces of research available on music-on-demand and usage data is not reachable since they belong to suppliers. It is also worth mentioning that listening to music is an act that does not necessitate constant focus and people can turn their attention more important duties such as their jobs, driving, exercising and using music as background filler. Therefore, tracking user behavior of music listeners is a tough task. Therefore, the author will use his own survey which allows him to make both qualitative and quantitative research. According to the responses of samples, there will be a comparison that will be drawn user behaviors before and after music-on-demand surfaced. With this paper, the author is aiming to fill a gap in the field and examine the future of music business from this aspect.

Research Part

In order to understand user habits, the author conducted a survey that consists eight questions to a sample of 276 participants which allowed them both to choose options and make comments. The author worked on surveys' statistical data and read user feedback on the music-on-demand services which makes the papers' research qualitative and quantitative.

The only demographic data that has been asked was their age and questions were answered anonymously. Although the age of the participants varies in between 18 and 50, the majority of the participants are in the ages between 20 and 30.
On the first question, participants asked how many hours they listen to music daily. Their responses varied but nearly 60 percent of the users listen to music less than 2 hours in the day, whereas less than 15 percent of the participants claim that they are listening to music more than 4 hours per day.

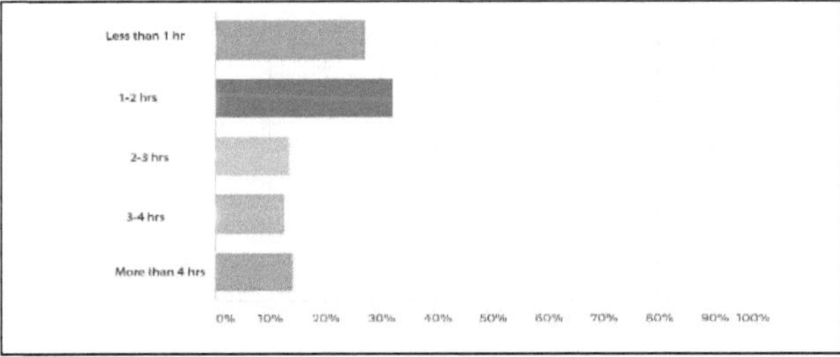

Figure1: How many hours are you listening to music?

One of the main concerns of this research was the question of whether the increasing numbers of music-on-demand services affecting the users' habits of owning the music they are listening to. On the survey, participants asked if they find it necessary to own the music they are listening to. The outcome was surprising as nearly 50 percent of the users still want to own their music on physical or digital formats and nearly 50 percent of the users do not find it necessary to own their music archive. On a commentary section, participants also asked when was the last time they purchased an album (digitally or physically). Only 67 out of 276 (24,27%) purchased an album within a year. The most accurate reading of this result is that it should be perceived as a personal preference of the music consumer when it comes to having an archive however it can be counted as a decrease since in the old ways of listening to music required owning the music whether it is in the physical format or digital format as you have to have a located .mp3 file in your computer in order to listen to it through your MP3 player. The existence of music-on-demand services prevented such necessity hence owning a music archive became optional and only depends on consumers' preference.

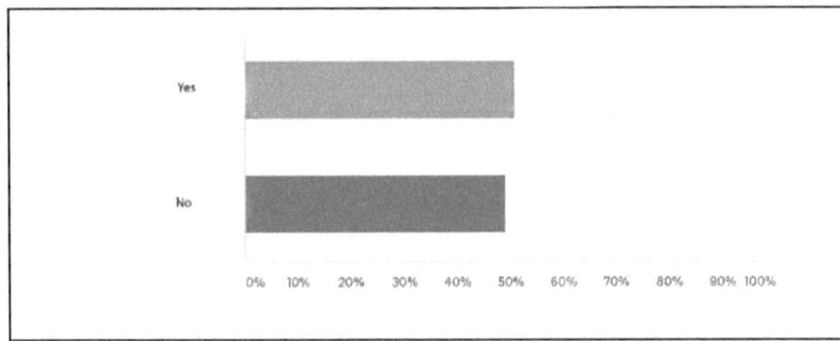

Figure 2: Is it necessary for you to own the music that you are listening to?

In order to examine the platform trends, participants asked which platforms they prefer while listening to music and allowed to choose more than one option. Their options were music-on-demand services such as Spotify and Apple Music, YouTube (although this research does not focus on YouTube and includes it as a music-on-demand service, YouTube obviously is one of the main channels of music consumers in our age and it is counted as a digital form of music consuming), illegal downloads (via torrent or mp3 sites), radio, vinyl, compact disks and cassettes. 223 out of 276 participants (82,90%) uses music-on-demand services and 189 out of 276 (70,26%) uses YouTube for listening to music. Although it is losing its old popularity, results show that radio is still one of the primary ways of music consuming as 104 participants out of 276 (38,66%) listen to music on the radio which makes it the third common way of music consuming after music-on-demand services and YouTube. Cassettes, compact disks, and vinyl can be perceived as a niche according to research responses as only 3 participants (1,12%) prefer cassettes, 25 participants (9,29%) and 33 participants (12,27%) prefers vinyl and compact disks respectively. 62 of the participants states that they are still using illegal downloads as a resource which can be assumed that it is declining with the prominence of music-on-demand services. This issue will be addressed again in the further sections of the research.

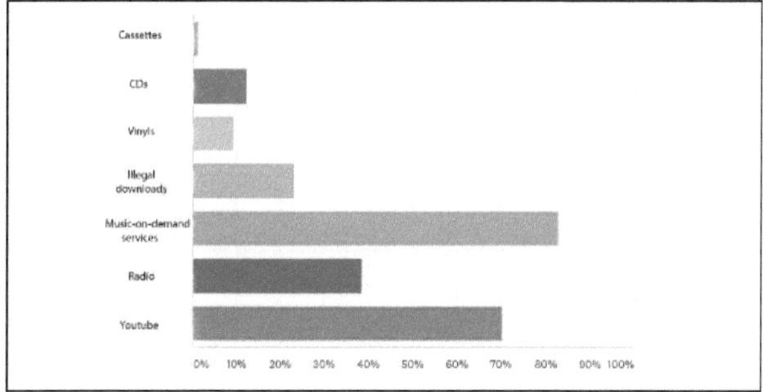

Figure 3: Which platform do you prefer while listening to music?

Another question was directed to people with the aim of gathering their habits while using music-on-demand applications and participants were allowed to choose more than one option. The majority of the users prefer switching song to song manually or with shuffle features of the services (179 out of 276 / 65,57%) over listening to an album entirely from beginning to end (107 out of 276 / 39,19%). 63,74% (174) of the users are listening to music on their own playlists whereas 48,35% (132) of them are listening to music from curated playlists by some other user or an algorithm. These data show that among the users of these applications, there is a tendency towards listening to music through playlists rather than albums. Users are either creating their own playlists from the music they love or exploring new music from curated playlists listening song-by-song. Another crucial data is that 64,84% (177) of the users claims that they are exploring new music through music-on-demand services and only 56 (20,51%) of them are sticking with the music they are already familiar with. This result can be interpreted as music-on-demand services functioning as a guide to new music rather than limiting its users' knowledge and forcing them on listening over and over same songs or artists.

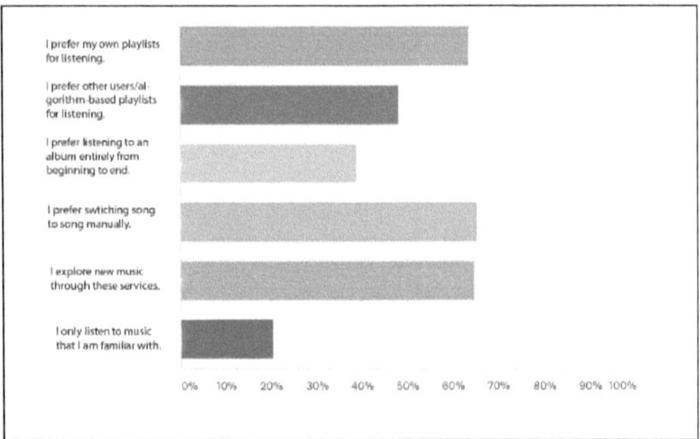

Figure 4: Habits of users on music-on-demand applications.

The final question of the research survey allows participants to make comments on how their listening habits changed with the entrance of music-on-demand services into their lives when it is compared to the past. This section of the survey gave the most important data and an insight into participants' habits and answered this papers' primary question: Are music streaming services affecting our listening habits? And if so, how?

Average music consumers mainly underlined the advantages of these services in their answers. Majority of the responses praised the services because of their library offerings and how they made them explore much more music when it is compared to the past. Instead of sticking with familiar artists or similar genres, users claimed that they are giving more chances to new artists and genres they are finding more challenging now without acting with preconception. Since they are allowed to listen to music offline in these apps, users are considering that they are owning much broader music archives in these days. According to this topic, user responses shows that the services not only made it easier to keep up with trending songs but also made easier to be in touch with older songs and albums. The convenience that music-on-demand services are offering accordingly increased the amount of time that people are spending on listening to music in a serious way as users asserting.

On the other hand, users that do not perceive themselves as 'casual audience' complained about their newly adopted habits that music-on-demand services bring. The people who consider themselves interested in music more than the casual audience gave feedback on how they are listening to albums entirely less day by day. The main concern of the group is the growing laziness on their music exploring process. There are several users among them who claimed that they are now only listening to half of a song and then skip it or finding it difficult to finish an entire album when it is compared to the pre-music-on-demand era. This is the major discontent among the users as I have also seen on the feedbacks of the people who consider themselves as 'casual audience'. There is a consensus among people who do not consider themselves as 'casual audience' on the convenience of algorithm-based playlists and radio features that's been offered by Spotify and Apple Music too, however, in a contradictory point of view they are feeling 'detained' by these features when it comes to exploring new music and described as 'addictive'. One of the participants told that: "The trends in the new music discovery are largely out of the hands of the user now. Suggested lists like "weekly discovery" offers really great songs, but we don't make researches on music like we did in the old days. We started to listen what we are suggested to listen now. In short, we got a little lazy. In the past, reaching music was something that necessitates effort, such as putting out a record or downloading from the internet. Now you do not have to toil to get good music. What's more, we can't determine our own style. Now I listen to music in a more careless way and it feels like music losing its value when it is constantly in my hands all the time".

One another common response is that the existence of these services made users quit downloading music from illegal channels and begin listening to music legally. It is claimed that dealing with downloading songs, converting and loading your music to music players is a time spending process and music-on-demand services are saving users' times. These comments are overlapping both with the statistics that served in theoretical part and the user research survey data that belong to the author.

Comments made it visible that people are now spending less amount of money on physical releases and less amount of time on the radio (a participant who stated that he or she is a radio DJ says: 'We are creating playlists from the songs that we've played on that day in our radio programs sharing them with our listeners through an official Spotify account just to reach out more people.') and they prefer spending their time and money on music-on-demand services. Numerous times, people repeated that they quit buying CDs (they referred CDs instead of albums in general and never mentioned vinyl or cassettes). One user claimed that in the past he or she was purchasing albums first and then listen to them but nowadays he or she only pays money to the physical releases of the albums he or she likes and in order to make a decision, he or she uses Spotify.

The results of the research are indeed drawing a parallel connection with the statistics that contributed to this paper and confirming the papers' main hypothesis that music-on-demand is changing users' listening habits. According to the users, the playlist system that's been introduced by music-on-demand services brought a convenience to the table as they find it much easier to explore new music now. Although there are some opposite opinions on them as some people complaining on how these playlists brought them a laziness, how exploring new music became much more effortless and missing that nostalgic feeling, the majority of the subscribers telling that music-on-demand services expanded their music knowledge and made their listening experience much funnier when it is compared to the past.

Many of the comments show that people became much more impatient over the music as they are stating that they are even finding it difficult now to finish the songs they are listening to. Listening to an album becoming a lost art day by day as consumers of these services find algorithm-based or user-curated playlists more appealing. Especially mood-based playlists are heavily praised which shows that such features now became the cornerstones of these services. This is the main problem that music-on-demand trend brought and it is the major change in the aspect of user behavior. Further comments will be made about this topic by the author on the conclusion part.

Music-on-demand services also changed the music business from the economic aspect. Users are stating that using these services is much cheaper than purchasing albums and they are very satisfied with the service they get since music-on-demand services are made it much easier to store users' music and saves their time as it eliminates the needless process of downloading and putting the files to their music players. The feedback shows that customers are happy that they are paying for the music they like and listening to it in a legal way. This is something beneficial for the artists and record labels as they get something instead of nothing for the effort they are spending.

Conclusion

The results were satisfactory as it provided all the answers to all of the concerns of this paper. Due to financial reasons and service quality, music consumers find it reasonable to pay the monthly subscription fee of music-on-demand services. This resulted with the end of illegal downloads. The same result may indicate that the decline in the physical album sales will most likely continue.
Future of the album format may also be in danger as user behavior strongly shifts through listening to playlists and there is a growing impatience regarding music among the consumers. Responses show that

people find it difficult to finish not only albums but even songs from beginning to end which can be regarded as the most crucial outcome of this research. This situation can be read as a serious threat to the album format. Some of the popular music artists seized on this trend and made innovative moves regarding the structures of albums and get praised by music critics as the latest release of hip-hop artist Drake, More Life, marketed as a playlist rather than an album and featured songs that were written and performed by other featured artists in the project. In a similar way, Humanz, the latest album of alternative hip-hop act Gorillaz, compared to Drake's More Life project by music critics because of its relatively long duration and songs that do not contain performances by Damon Albarn (British musician and head of the Gorillaz project) although it was not supposed to be seen as a playlist album format.

More than 80% of the participants stated they are listening to music on streaming services whereas more than 70% of the participants use YouTube as a consuming channel which can be counted as a digital way of consuming music. Although radio is still the third most common way to consume music, its popularity is declining and slowly losing its spot to digital streaming services according to survey results. The research indicates that music-on-demand services became the primary resource of music exploration and have taken over radio's place. Instead of listening to the verbal curations of radio DJ's, people find it relatively attractive algorithm-based playlists or the radio features of the music-on-demand services and continues to listen to music without breaks.

When participants were asked when did they started using 'digital platforms' for music consuming their responses varied as some of the people only perceived music-on-demand services as 'digital platforms' whereas other users counted platforms such as Napster and Kazaa which allowed people downloading music illegally and responded accordingly. The situation created a gap in the research and as a result, the author was not able to measure the responses in a meaningful way.

A further research could be made on what will future brings to album format in music and a psychologic research on the user behavior can be initiated and the tendency towards users' impatience while listening to music can be explained in detail.

Acknowledgement

This paper was written within the scope of the undergraduate course "Advanced Issues in Communication Studies" (Fall 2017-2018) of the Department of Communication and Design at Bilkent University which was directed by Dr. Dr. Lutz Peschke.

References

Gürmeriç, Can (2017): Music Streaming Services Against Traditional Music Industry: Success of Streaming Services in the Case of Spotify and Apple. In Lutz Peschke (Ed.), *New Media Between User Generated Content and Professionalism*. Saarbrücken: Lambert Academic Publishing.

Goldmann, Mikael / Kreitz, Gunnar (2011, August): Measurements on the spotify peer-assisted music-on-demand streaming system. In: *Peer-to-Peer Computing (P2P), 2011 IEEE International Conference on* (pp. 206-211). IEEE. Retrieved from https://ieeexplore.ieee.org/abstract/document/6038737/ Accessed on Apr. 10, 2018.

Kreitz, Gunnar / Niemela, Fredrik (2010, August): Spotify--large scale, low latency, P2P music-on-demand streaming. In *Peer-to-Peer Computing (P2P), 2010 IEEE Tenth International Conference on* (pp. 1-10). IEEE. Retrieved from https://ieeexplore.ieee.org/abstract/document/5569963/ Accessed on Apr. 10, 2018.

Morris, Jeremy Wade / Powers, Devon (2015): Control, curation and musical experience in streaming music services. *Creative Industries Journal, 8*(2), 106-122. Retrieved from https://www.tandfonline.com/doi/abs/10.1080/17510694.2015.1090222 Accessed on Apr. 10, 2018.

Zhang, Boxun/Kreitz, Gunnar/Isaksson, Marcus/Ubillos, Javier/Urdaneta, Guido/Pouwelse, Johan A./Epema, Dick (2013, April): Understanding user behavior in spotify. In: *INFOCOM, 2013 Proceedings IEEE* (pp. 220-224).

IEEE. Retrieved from
https://ieeexplore.ieee.org/abstract/document/6566767/ Accessed on Apr.
10, 2018.

Impact of Social Media Activities on Maintaining Brand Reputation

Korcan Hekimoğlu[*]

Social media platforms can be considered as a place to socialize and create connections between brands and prospective customers. In recent years, social media doubled its significant position in companies' marketing operations because of its wide use and potential of advertising. Managing and controlling their position in that area is essential for the success of companies' overall marketing operations. It is clear that all global players are trying to impress their potential and existing customers through their social media channels. Thus, to reach customers in an effective way, companies are implementing various strategies in their social media channels. This research discusses the potential effects of how social media channels (Twitter, Facebook, and Instagram) influence branding, creation of a brand image, and loyalty over time. In this research, various cases were examined in order to show the significance of effective or proper implementation of overall social media plans. Some ineffective and improper use of social media channels were examined. As a further examination, a structured analysis based on Google Search data and Twitter was used in order to understand the consumer's perspective related to importance of social media channels' in the way of influencing brand reputation.

[*] Korcan Hekimoğlu, Bilkent University, Department of Communication and Design. Ankara/Turkey

Research Question: To what extent, can the management of a crisis situation in social media can affect the brand reputation?

Keywords: Social media, social media marketing, brand reputation, social media crisis, crisis situation, social media strategy.

Introduction

Social media has changed the understanding of communication and the way brands communicate with people. Without any geographical limitation, users are able to interact, express their opinions, and discuss certain things through social media platforms such as Twitter, Facebook, Tumblr etc. In these channels, news and information are spreading all over the planet instantly. People share any type of information without any avoidance, and share information about their personal interests, relationships, favorite brands etc. With this new type of information flow, companies need to come up with a new way of measuring and controlling for their brands' health. Social media platforms have a huge role and potential in the way of shaping a brand's position in the consumers' mind. In addition to that, other customers' opinions are also shaping potential customers' mind and brands' perception. While making their decisions, consumers are highly affected by a brand's operations in social media in their "evaluation" stage. Also, with social media platforms, a new type of engagement started to emerge between brands and consumers. Because of the popularity and capabilities of social media in connecting people and brands, many researchers are advising businesses to improve their appearances in these channels and take the benefits of these platforms (Kaplan / Haenlein 2010). Through social media platforms, companies are able to create a unique type of relationship between their brands and customers. Also, the companies' goal is to use social media platforms for influencing people in their decision making and in long run to create brand loyalty for their products.

The traditional ways of measuring brand are no longer valid under today's huge information traffic and social media age. Today, consumers are no longer loyal to their brands and their perception of a brand is always changing. The success of social media operations is also dependent on well-established relationships between brands and customers. In addition to that, engagement with the customer is another key element of the successful social media implementation. This research focuses on the significance of managing a brand's reputation and importance of branding in social media specifically. It is a fact that many of the companies are losing their potential customers as a result of huge amount of user interaction and complains at the same time. Under certain situations, wrong management of such operations can lead to irreversible faults such as the United Airlines' PR crisis. For creating brand equity and positive brand image, companies need to take advantage of specific measuring tool and develop their strategies in the light of these elements. For this research, the crisis cases of the three companies were selected specifically for presenting the significance of managing social media operations for the overall success of company operations.

Hypothesis 1. There is a strong relationship between Google Search data peaks and crisis periods of brands.

Hypothesis 2. Doing nothing under certain crisis situations or poor management can lead to spread of the crisis.

Hypothesis 3. Having a brand community in social media platforms can influence brand operations in a positive way.

Hypothesis 4. Improper application of social media operations can lead financial loss for companies.

Theoretical Framework

A. The Consumer Decision Journey Model

The Consumer Decision Journey model developed as a result of traditional Funnel Metaphor's limitation in terms of presenting consumers' post-purchase behavior and its oversimplified look to the buying process. For the Funnel Metaphor, consumers start their buying process by examining many brands or services and they narrow their brands to fewer brands. This behavior is followed by buying decision. This traditional model was so limited because of not focusing on the after-sale behavior of the consumer. Due to inability to explain significant points related to purchase behavior of consumers, the Consumer Decision Journey (CDJ) Model was developed by former McKinsey employee D. Court and his colleagues (Hudson / Thal 2013).

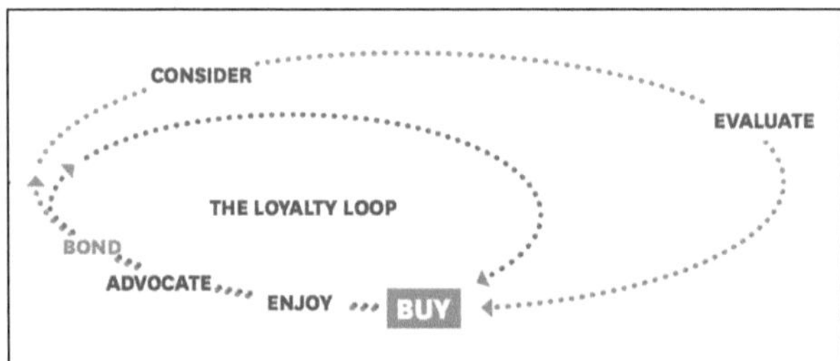

Figure 1: The Consumer Decision Journey Model (CDJ) (Based on Court et al., 2009)

In this model, instead of narrowing their choices, consumers add or subtract brands to an evaluation group in their evaluation phase. For CDJ Model, after the purchase behavior, consumers are tending to create a deeper connection with the brand through various channels such as Twitter, Facebook, online forums etc. Depending on the consumer's pleasure about service or product, they can tend to advocate product in various channels including social media and word of mouth. Under strong relationship conditions, an enjoy - advocate - buy loop can be established with the consumers.

This model is notably significant for this research because of its potential about explaining and clarifying the missing points related to the establishment of brand equity and trust affair between brands and consumers. Also, social media channels are highly preferred for the "Consider" stage in influencing consumers and driving traffic to companies' web page for potential sale. In addition to that, companies are using social media channels for reaching markets and providing information to their potential consumers in their "Evaluation" stage. To clarify, this model highlights the significance of social media and its engagement ability in the way of consumer's buying decision process. It is certain that social media channels can be used for establishing strong relationships and durability between consumers and companies.

B. Model of The Effects of Brand Community (On Social Media)

Social media channels are allowing companies to constitute a unique type of affair between brands and consumers. This model centers around the argument of brand communities established in social media channels have a positive effect on overall customer and brand relations in the way of developing brand trust and brand loyalty under perfect management. According to various conducted studies, consumers have a desire for social interaction through social media channels such as Twitter, Facebook Groups, forums etc. as a fraction of their psychological needs. Thus, they are tending to create a social tie between different members of the social media channels.

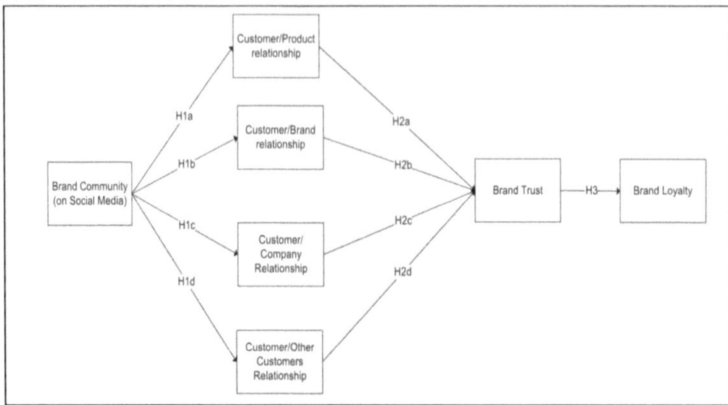

Figure 2: Model of The Effects of Brand Community on Social Media (Laroche, Habibi & Richard 2013)

We are able to define the power of social media as being a considerably efficient communication tool, as a powerful apparatus for shaping consumer's perception and combining different/similar clusters of people in the same environment. Doubtless to say, one of the goals of brands through social media is creating a great community with great relationships reciprocally. The establishment of strong relationships can result in customer loyalty in return for companies. Also, trust is one of the keys to the building and sustaining of customer loyalty. This model will be useful for illustrating the significance of sustaining and building a "trust" relationship with our customer in social media channels. By strengthening their relationships, companies can establish a brand equity and brand loyalty in the long-term period. It is certain that management and control of a brand's image in social media channels are essential for the long-term success of overall company operations and building better affair with publics.

C. Three Elements for Effective Social Media Implementation

Web 2.0 and emergence of new social media channels created a new environment with dozens of opportunities for companies. Firms are able to develop their own operations based on their inferences from these platforms, and they are able to interact with their customers and environments without any intermediary. It is certain that social media channels are not a basic "value creator" for firms. By using the strategy effectively and implementing it in a proper way, companies can add value to their brand through social media channels. The table of "How Virtual Customer Environments Create Value" is quite informative about value generation of various firm operations in the social media ecosystem. Especially with branding (advertising, PR, content delivery), customer service and support, companies can create a great source of value and build brand equity and reputation in the long term.

Activity Supported	Source of Value
Branding (advertising, PR, content delivery)	Drive traffic, viral marketing, customer loyalty and retention
Sales (includes "call to action" — e.g., link to purchase item)	Revenue
Customer service and support	Cost savings, revenue, customer satisfaction
Product Development	Revenue

Table 1: How Virtual Customer Environments Create Value (Culnan, McHugh & Zubillaga 2010)

To clarify, social media activities will contribute brand reputation in a desired way with proper branding and customer service activities. In addition to that, companies need to carefully develop their social media implementation strategy based on three compelling elements: *mindful adaptation, community building, and absorptive capacity* respectively.

Selection of the social media channel is crucial to the success of the overall operation. If we examine carefully, each of the Fortune 500 company has their own social media use behavior. In terms of average, these leading companies have adopted almost more than one social media platform. Only seven percent of these companies are using the most known four social media channels (Li 2008). Thus, choice of social media channel differs considerably among companies based on their position and branding strategy.

Mindful Adoption	Community Building	Absorptive Capacity
Adoption of social media channel based on organization's culture, target customers, and business adoption.	Continuous engaging content.	Assigning responsibility to designated employees or departments for monitoring social media.
Developing quantitate and qualitative metrics for measuring the value of social media applications.	Incentives for participation.	For structured messages, integrating social media applications with existing web services.
Addressing risk management issues, including security and privacy issues.	Balancing freedom with control and accountability.	Share of information across the firm.

Table 2: Elements of Effective Social Media Implementation

The first element of related argument focuses on the "Mindful Adaptation Decisions". This basically deals with the appropriate platform selection, control and measure of it, and risk management. Doubtless, to say, social media platforms can create a problematic situation for a company as a result of a large number of employee's collaboration on behalf of the firm. Also, consumer complaints about the company is another problem related to the case. In the case of improper implementation, an image in social media can harm the overall brand image and loyalty of customers. The case of a passenger removed from United Airlines and the companies' social media actions can be considered as a great example of improper implementation of social media strategy.

The second central element of argument highlights the significance of "Community Building" in social media channels. It is certain that opening a Twitter or Facebook account is not enough for attracting people and expecting from them to engage. The third element of the argument focuses on the "Absorptive Capacity". To clarify, understanding people and their complaints can be helpful for the development of strong and long-lasting relationships.

"The Elements of Effective Social Media Implementation" is enormously significant for the success of overall social media operations. Under certain cases, wrong management of these operations can result in failure in terms of brand image and brand loyalty. As indicated before, most of the customers are tending to engage with their brand. By combining our overall strategy based on these elements, we are able to get better outcomes from our social media channels. This concept will be useful for in the way of clarifying the importance of social media channels' management for sustaining brand image and reputation.

Data and Methods

The selected method of examination for this research is content analysis. Content analysis is 'a technique for examining information and content, in written or symbolic materials' (Neuman 1997). This study has three different units of analysis. The first analysis method is based on Google Search Trends data of related brands (Uber, United Airlines, and PepsiCo). To clarify, Google Trends is a real-time daily and weekly index of the volume of queries that users enter into Google Search Engine (Choi & Varian 2012). This type of analysis selected in order to find meaningful peaks and changes in Google Search results of selected brands and their match with the crisis dates of these brands. These Google Trends findings will be examined in three sub categories: data peaks in data set based on dates and weeks, search related topics of users, and interest by region respectively. Different time ranges will be used for different brands. For Uber and United Airlines, this time range is limited with 60 to 200 dates respectively. For Pepsi, one-year period starting from 15 December 2016 will be used for Google Trends examination. The rationale behind selection of one-year period for Pepsi is, their products are available in more than 200 countries and territories (PepsiCo).

The second phase of analysis is based on peak dates of Google Search Results of this three brands and peak dates' reflections on their Twitter environment. Twitter's instant and conversation based interaction ability with users and brands are making able to see a negative or positive image of a brand. For peak dates, top 100 prominent tweets from Twitter's Advanced Search Tool will be selected. Prominent tweets will be examined based on Perception and Engagement Model in order to understand these brands' image in Twitter and users' perception related to the brand. As the third unit of analysis, users most used key terms, their hashtag and image use and their behavior, in general, will be carefully examined in the light of Perception and Engagement Model.

Examination of Google Trends Data of Selected Brands

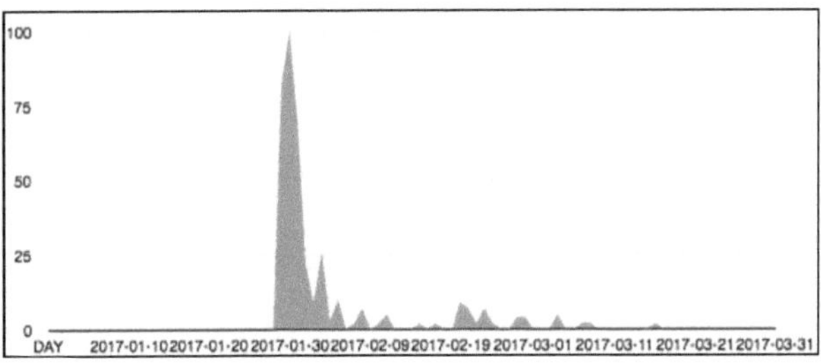

Figure 3: #DeleteUber Worldwide Google Search Trends (Google Trends 2017)

In the selected period, starting from 1 January 2017 to 31 March 2017, Uber Technologies, Inc. (Uber), were faced with two major crises: President Trump's travel bans and their response to this action and leaks of a former women employee about gender discrimination in Uber. It is a fact that Twitter became the leading social platform for people complains in this period. To clarify, Uber's response to protesters in J.F. Kennedy Airport about surge pricing, turned to a social media crisis with #DeleteUber stream in 29th January. By using #DeleteUber in their tweets, people shared their own complains, stories, and ideas about the company. People considered this action of Uber as supporting President Donald Trump's Muslim Travel Ban. As a fraction of this, people complain and #DeleteUber search results reached a peak by 30 January 2017. After a certain point, sharing the screenshots of deleting Uber Application from their mobile phones became a stream on Twitter. In just 24 hours, #DeleteUber tweeted by more than 1000 users and they shared almost 1388 tweets about the issue. This amount of tweet accounts for more than 30 million impressions in overall. According to Google Trends data in given period, for 30th January 2017, we have the highest Google Search interaction. Google Trends data peak of #DeleteUber completely overlaps with the Uber's scandal data.

Table 3 illustrates the interest by region for #DeleteUber in Google Search. It certain that, in all regions of interest, Uber Company has operations. Also, Singapore is leading country in interest (As a result of being a small territory compared to the US).

Country	Interest
Singapore	100
United States	91
South Africa	90
Canada	50
Philippines	45
Australia	30
France	18
United Kingdom	17
Netherlands	14
Thailand	13
Germany	8
Mexico	7
India	5
Japan	4
Brazil	3

Table 3: Table 3. Interest by Region for #DeleteUber.

Category: All categories	Interest
TOP	
Uber	100
Donald Trump	20
Muslim	5
Lyft	5
RISING	
Uber	Breakout
Donald Trump	Breakout
Muslim	Breakout
Lyft	Breakout

Table 4: Related Searches for #DeleteUber.

Table 4 shows the other related searches of users based on #DeleteUber. The most related search of users is "Uber" key term. Other than that, after searching #DeleteUber, a considerable number of users tended to search "Donald Trump". In addition to that, users also searched for Muslim" term and "Lyft" which is the main competitor of Uber Company.

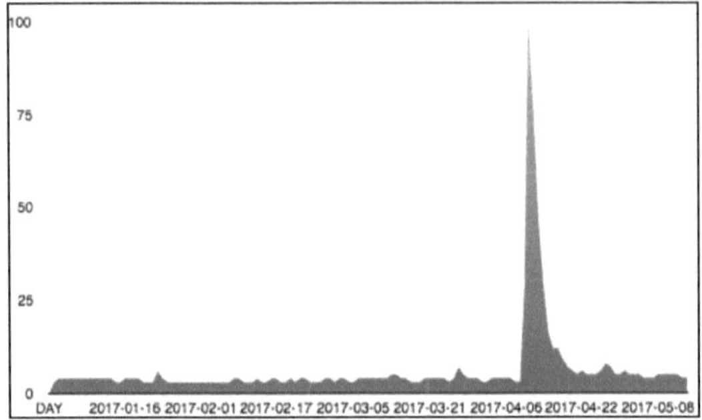

Figure 4: United Airlines Worldwide Google Search Trends (Google Trends 2017)

Figure 4 illustrates the Google Search Trends of United Airlines, starting from 1 January 2017 to 15 May 2017. This period is specifically selected because of the purpose of seeing the effect of United Airlines' public relations crisis in Google Search results in the middle term. On 9 April 2017, a passenger was violently removed from United Airlines Flight 3411. Mainly on Twitter, people shared their complaints and waited for an apology from the company. After the release of an internal letter of United Airlines CEO on 10th April, about his support to his employees, this crisis became a global crisis for the company. After this, United Airlines lost almost 1 billion US Dollars from its market value. For the date 11 April 2017, we have the highest Google Search interaction of users from 45 different countries, including territories and counties with no United Airlines flight.

Table 5 shows the related searches of users who searched United Airlines using Google Search. For this period, we have no significant change in users related searches for United Airlines. Users tended to search other airlines, airport, and stock information.

Category: All categories	
TOP	
United Airlines	100
Flight	10
American Airlines	5
Stock	5
Airline	5
Delta Air Lines	5
Southwest Airlines	5
Airports	5

Table 5: Related Searches for United Airlines (Google Trends 2017)

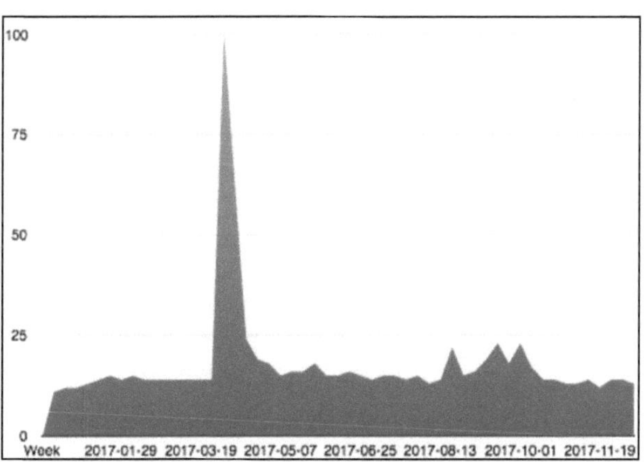

Figure 4: Pepsi Worldwide Google Search Trends.

Figure 4 shows the Google Search data trends of Pepsi starting from 15 December 2016 to 15 December 2017. This period is specifically selected for examining the international effect of their Kendall Jenner featured advertisement and for seeing their overall company search trends. This advertisement was criticized widely because of its reference to the Black Lives Matter movement. After criticisms which Pepsi Company did not expect, they pulled advertisement from a stream and apologized for this advertisement immediately. For the date 4 April 2017, we have the highest search result peak for the whole year period. This peak date matches exactly with the crisis date of Pepsi Company. Only after three-week period, Pepsi's search trends turned into its usual flow.

Category: All categories	
TOP	
Pepsi	100
Advertising	10
Kendall Jenner	10
Coca-Cola	10
PepsiCo	10
Cola	5
Pepsi Center	5
Pepsi Max	5
RISING	
Kendall Jenner	Breakout
Sky News	Breakout
Contamination	Breakout
Battle of the Bands	Breakout
AIDS	Breakout
HIV	+4,550%

Kylie Jenner	+3,650%
Controversy	+2,600%
United Airlines	+1,550%
Protest	+1,400%

Table 6: Related Searches for Pepsi (Google Trends 2017).

Table 6 shows the "Pepsi" related searches of users using Google Search. It is fact that "Advertising" and "Kendall Jenner" search terms are prominent in overall search even in one-year period. Other than that, users also searched about competitor "Coca-Cola" and other products of Pepsi such as "Pepsi Max".

A further noteworthy thing is that the "Kendall Jenner" search term made a considerable search breakout in relation with "Pepsi". One significant thing is that users also searched for "United Airlines", after searching "Pepsi" term. This situation can be considered as, both crisis happened so nearly to each other. It can be considered that people may have caught a connection between these two events.

Examination of Twitter Data (Based on Google Trends Peaks)

A. #DeleteUber and Its Reflections on Twitter

According to Google Trends data in given period, on 30th January 2017, we have the highest Google Search interaction for #DeleteUber. On 30th January, the top 100 users' tweets selected based on their prominence in Twitter's Advanced Search Tool. While examining, the randomness of tweets was also taken into account. Based on their use of words, positive or negative comment use, #DeleteUber or other hashtag use, using the competitor's name such as Lyft and sharing a screen shot of deleting Uber application also taken into account for the examination.

DIFFERENT USED TAGS	
#StopPresidentBannon	More Than Five
#NoMoreUber	
#BoycottUber	More Than Five
#CorporateCollabrator	More Than Five
#Resist	
#TheResistance	
#StayWake	
#DeleteStupidty	
#DeleteLyft	
#NoBanNoWall	

Table 7: Different Used Tags (Other Than #DeleteUber) (Google Trends 2017)

Selected examination categories for tweets: Tag use (Other than #DeleteUber), Image Share, Sharing Meme, Sharing Screen Shots, Negative Comments, Positive Comments.

Table 7 shows the different used hashtags of users. Mostly, users used #StopPresidentBannon hashtags in their tweets. This can be considered as the fraction of users' comments related to Uber's CEO's political affinity to President Donald Trump.

Other than that, Twitter users mostly used #BoycottUber and #CorporateCollabrator hashtags. Based on this inclination of users, it can be considered that users are mostly complaining about the political affinity of Uber.

Category	Number
Image Share	4
Share of Screen Shots	5
Article or Link Share	43
Mentioning Competitors	19
Negative Comments	25
Positive Comments	13
Sharing Meme (Entertaining Content)	4

Table 8: Examination of #DeleteUber based on categories (Twitter 2017)

Table 8 illustrates the other categories for the examination of #DeleteUber and activities of prominent 100 tweets on 30th January 2017. 43 of the 100 tweets shared with an article or link. In these 43 tweets, users tended to tweet news article of Uber.

B. United Airlines PR Crisis and Its Reflections on Twitter

On 9 April 2017, a passenger was violently removed from United Airlines Flight 3411 because of the overbooking problem. After the release of an internal letter from the United Airlines CEO on 10th April, about his support to his employees, this crisis became a global crisis for the company. This situation was highly criticized in all social media sites, especially on Twitter, it became viral. People shared their ideas related to the issue and criticized United Airlines for their action. According to Google Trends data in the related period, for the 11 April 2017, we have the highest Google Search interaction for United Airlines. For 11th April 2017, the top 100 users' tweets selected based on their prominence in Twitter's Advanced Search Tool. While examining, randomness also is taken into account. Based on users use of words, positive or negative comments, competitors' names such as American, Delta, and sharing images or screenshots related to United Airlines also taken into account for the examination.

DIFFERENT USED TAGS	Number
#FlyWithFriendlySkies	1
#United3411	1
#Terrible	1
#FlyTheFriendItSkies	1

Table 9: Different Used Tags (Twitter 2017).

Table 9 shows the different used hashtags in top 100 tweets with "United Airlines" key term. It is fact that, hashtag use of users remained so limited compared to other elements of analysis.

Category	Number
Image Share	20
Share of Screen Shots	2
Article or Link Share	9
Mentioning Competitors	3
Negative Comments	38
Positive Comments	-
Sharing Meme (Entertaining Content)	15

Table 10: Examination Categories of Tweets (Twitter 2017).

Table 10 shows the examination categories for overall selected 100 tweets. It is certain that most of the users made a negative comment related to United Airlines in their tweets. Other than negative comments, a certain number of users shared image and video in their tweets about the issue. Also, users sent much entertaining content, mostly "meme" in their tweets. This action of users can be attributed to the tragedy of the situation. It is fact that users tended to share video and image content of United airlines with the other users.

C. Pepsi Kendall Jenner Advertisement Crisis and Its Reflections on Twitter

Category	Number
Image Share	14
Share of Screen Shots	0
Article or Link Share	4
Mentioning Competitors	6
Negative Comments	29
Positive Comments	6
Sharing Mem (Entertaining Content	15

Table 11: Examination Categories of Tweets for Pepsi (Twitter 2017).

According to Google Trends data in one-year period, on 4 April 2017, we have the highest Google Search interaction for Pepsi. On 4 April 2017, the top 100 tweets selected based on their prominence in Twitter's Advanced Search Tool. While examining, the randomness of tweets also taken into account. In the analysis, users use of words, their positive or negative comments, hashtag use, mentioning competitors' names such as Coke, and sharing an image or video related to Pepsi also taken into account for the examination.

For the Pepsi Kendall Jenner advertisement case, users tweeted mostly with negative comments. Other than that, a considerable number of users just used texts without any image or hashtags. More than 30% of users tweeted with image or video in their tweets. It is fact that no one shared any screenshot or any related content in their tweet.

Results and Discussion

As predicted, under crisis situations, Google Search interactions for brands are dramatically increasing. It certain that, under crisis situations, a brand becomes completely vulnerable because of the potential of searches (recommended, and trending searches) and viral side of the issue. People tend to search more for a brand in a crisis situation. For selected three cases, Google Search data peaks are completely parallel with their crisis situation dates.

Google Search data of "#DeleteUber" shows us the most searches were done in 15 countries where Uber is actively operating. Other than that, consumers tended to search "Donald Trump" and "Muslim" key terms after searching "#DeleteUber". This presents us the point of view of the users against Uber's action towards to President Trump's Muslim travel ban. Likewise, people tended to search for the main competitor of Uber using Google Search: Lyft. The following conclusion can be drawn from this: as a consequence of the damage of trust environment, people tended to search for an alternative to Uber's service. As indicated in the Consumer Decision Journey Model, Uber became unsuccessful about establishing a "trust" relationship with customers and destroyed the "loyalty loop" of its present customers.

When we look at the Twitter activity for Uber, in selected 100 tweets, users mostly tended to share articles related to Uber's action. 19 out of 100 users have clearly stated that they will prefer Uber's main rival Lyft, as a result of Uber's action. Also, people stated 25 negatives and 13 positive comments about Uber. In the positive comments made by users, they pointed out, they could not abandon Uber for such a reason. A further noteworthy thing is that all of the tags used for Uber are tagged with negative comments about Uber.

It is certain that, according to Model of the Effects of Brand Community Model, it can be seen that the shares of different users related to Uber are triggered by other users. For such cases, Uber has no established brand community. More than 50 of the users have shared articles and links about Uber many times. Apart from that, 5 out of 100 users shared a screen shot of deleted Uber application in their tweets. Under careful examination, it is seen that the atmosphere of confidence for Uber was considerably damaged.

Based on the Engagement Model, it can be considered that #DeleteUber has a viral character and the event is not only shared in English but also in different languages including Spanish. In addition to that, Uber did not communicate with customers who comment negatively or communicate their complaints. Taking the whole situation into consideration, the attitude that portrayed by Uber on the day, resulted has resulted in incredible complaints. As a result of not having their own community and does not choose to interact with users, users tended to tweet about Uber's main competitor Lyft, and share of screenshots.

For United Airlines, Google Search data peaks are perfectly parallel with the period of United Airlines' public relations crisis. When we examine the related searches for United Airlines, there is no any different standing search in Google data. Mainly, users tended to search other airlines, airports, and stock information. On the other hand, Twitter interactions for United Airlines is contrasting with Google Search data. It is fact that 38 out of 100 users tweeted negative comments related to United Airlines. Compared to Uber's case, there are no any positive commented tweets about United Airlines. As a general trend, people tended to share images and videos about a passenger violently removed from a flight. Only in 9 out of 100 tweets, people tweeted an article or link related to issue. Also, in 15 out of 100, users shared entertaining content in their tweets. This action can be attributed to the tragedy of the situation.

When we examine this case in the light of the Model of the Effects of Brand Community, it can deduct that the shares of different users related to United Airlines are triggered by other users. Even if, United Airlines have a support team for replying comments related to airlines, for this case, they stopped sharing any related content. Also, they have no community for such situations, and also for promoting their brand. In terms of the Engagement Model, this case gained a viral character after a certain point. However, based on Google Search data, this crisis has lost its significance in the middle term. While analyzing, there is no any significant related search and peaks in Google Search data observed.

For Pepsi, one-year period starting from 15 December 2016 to 15 December 2017 was specifically selected for examining the international effect of Pepsi's Kendall Jenner featured advertisement. For the week 2 to 8 April 2017, we faced with the highest Google Search interaction for Pepsi. This peak period directly matches with the advertisement's release period. It is fact that, only after three weeks of considerable Google Search data, searches turned to its normal flow. As a mechanism, Google Trends shorting related searches based on time range and the highest rate of search. In one-year period "related search" data, terms such as "advertising", the "Kendall Jenner" are the prominent ones. This situation shows us that, Kendall Jenner featured advertisement had a serious impact on the Pepsi brand even within one-year period. Another significant thing related to Google Search data of Pepsi is that people also searched for "United Airlines" in relation to Pepsi searches. This case can be considered as people may found some kind of similarity in the situation of United Airlines and Pepsi.

According to Twitter data of Pepsi, there is no significant tweet interaction of users compared to both United Airlines and Uber. For the Kendall Jenner advertisement, 29 out of 100 tweets were negative commented. As a general trend, people complained about Pepsi's advertisement's reference to the "Black Lives Matter" Movement. 14 out of 100 tweets were shared with an image. Also, 15 out of 100 tweets were shared with entertaining content. In addition to that, 30% of tweets, tweeted with an image or video. This shows us the people's willingness about sharing advertisement's content even if, it is removed from YouTube and other platforms.

Overall, Pepsi failed in managing its Twitter operations. People continued sharing advertisement video for three weeks. Also, Pepsi has no brand community and significant engagement with Twitter users. Pepsi failed about engaging users with its content in order to eliminate racist arguments related to the brand.

Based on the Three Elements of Effective Social Media Implementation, Pepsi failed to represent an effective branding for its product and also, they failed in creating customer satisfaction. To clarify, these actions affected Pepsi brand in a negative way. In addition to that, Pepsi could not balance freedom of users with control and accountability.

Conclusion

This research was designed to clarify the significance of managing and controlling social media operations for creating a brand image and loyalty in the long run. As predicted in the hypothesis, there is a strong relationship with Google Search data peaks and brands' crisis situations. For all selected cases, Google Search data peaks represented the crisis situations' occurrence period. Also, a "related search" data of users was used for finding meaningful correlations between brand's image and crisis situation.

"#DeleteUber" movement can be considered as a great example for the poor management of social media operations. By the share of over 1000 Twitter accounts in one day, "#DeleteUber" movement gained a viral effect and resulted in 200,000 customer losses for Uber in just a few days. As noted earlier in hypothesis, poor engagement and having no brand community can result in misunderstanding for many of users. It is certain that social media is a powerful tool for shaping customers' perception and creating relationships in long run.

United Airline's search results peaks are perfectly parallel with their crisis period. They faced difficulty mainly on Twitter. An enormous number of users shared negative comments related to the airline. For only in United Airlines case, there is no any positive commented tweet. As a general trend, people shared images and videos about a passenger violently removed from the flight. This viral effect of the content and poor management of the situation lead to loss of almost 1 billion US Dollar for United Airlines. As indicated in the Consumer Decision Journey Model, consumer's dissatisfaction about United Airlines lead to a share of opponent opinion in various channels including word of mouth.

As we observe from the Google Search data, Pepsi experienced a significant search interaction in Google for 2 to 8 April 2017 period. In one-year period, still terms such as "Advertising" and "Kendall Jenner" remain as the most prominent related searches of people. Important thing related to Google Search data of Pepsi is, people also searched for "United Airlines" in relation to Pepsi searches. This situation can be considered as, people's consideration about the similarity in the situation of Pepsi and United Airlines.

In all examined cases, companies failed to implement the most basic social media strategies in their operations. Overall, they preferred sharing no content and making no engagement in the first levels of crisis. Having no brand community on social media platforms also affected their brand in a negative way. As a result of this, this crisis became viral in hours. In addition to that, Google Search trends of users also reflected the crisis starting period and its development exactly.

Acknowledgement

This paper was written within the scope of the undergraduate course "Advanced Issues in Communication Studies" (Fall 2017-2018) of the Department of Communication and Design at Bilkent University which was directed by Dr. Dr. Lutz Peschke.

References

Choi, Hyunyoung / Varian, Hal (2012): Predicting the present with Google Trends. *Economic Record, 88*(s1), 2-9. Retrieved from https://onlinelibrary.wiley.com/doi/full/10.1111/j.1475-4932.2012.00809.x Accessed on Apr. 10, 2018

Culnan, Mary J. / McHugh, Patrick J. / Zubillaga, Jesus I. (2010): How large US companies can use Twitter and other social media to gain business value. *MIS Quarterly Executive, 9*(4). Retrieved from https://onlinelibrary.wiley.com/doi/full/10.1111/j.1475-4932.2012.00809.x Accessed on Apr. 10, 2018

Edelman, David C. (2010): Branding in the digital age. *Harvard business review, 88*(12), 62-69. Retrieved from http://saberfazermarketing.com/wp-content/uploads/2011/10/Branding-in-the-Digital-Age.pdf Accessed on Apr. 10, 2018

Hudson, Simon / Thal, Karon (2013): The impact of social media on the consumer decision process: Implications for tourism marketing. *Journal of Travel & Tourism Marketing, 30*(1-2), 156-160. Retrieved from https://www.tandfonline.com/doi/abs/10.1080/10548408.2013.751276 Accessed on Apr. 10, 2018

Kaplan, Andreas M. / Haenlein, Michael (2010): Users of the world, unite! The challenges and opportunities of Social Media. *Business horizons, 53*(1), 59-68. Retrieved from http://michaelhaenlein.com/Publications/Kaplan,%20Andreas%20-%20Users%20of%20the%20world,%20unite.pdf Accessed on Apr. 10, 2018

Laroche, Michel / Habibi, Mohammad Reza / Richard, Marie-Odile (2013): To be or not to be in social media: How brand loyalty is affected by social media?. *International Journal of Information Management, 33*(1), 76-82. Retrieved from http://shop.tarjomeplus.com/Uploads/site-1/DownloadDoc/557.pdf Accessed on Apr. 10, 2018

Li, Charlene (2010): Groundswell. Winning in a world transformed by social technologies. *Strategic Direction, 26*(8). Retrieved from https://doi.org/10.1108/sd.2010.05626hae.002 Accessed on Apr. 10, 2018

Neuman, Lawrence W. (1992): *Social Research Methods: Qualitative and Quantitative Approaches.* (3rd ed.) Boston: Allyn & Bacon.

Social Media Engagement and Perception as a Measure of Brand Health (Rep. No. 1). (2015). New York: Tracx Attention.

About the Authors

Gizem BAHÇECİOĞLU was born in 1995 in Kayseri, Turkey. She took her elementary education at TED Kayseri College. Later, she graduated from Bilkent High School in 2013. She studied at Bilkent University Faculty of Communication and Design Department and graduated in 2018.She did her internships in Ankara. She completed her first internship in NTV Ankara. For the second internship, she worked in Ness Iletisim ve Danismanlik as a PR person. In NTV, she worked for writing news and making interviews. In Ness Iletisim, she worked for social media accounts of clients. She also worked for writing bulletins. In upcoming period, she is planning to focus on PR and advertising.

Kardem DİM was born in 1995 in Alanya. She graduated from American Collegiate Institute in İzmir in 2014 and got accepted to Bilkent University, Communication and Design Department in 2014. She had studied in Communication and Design Department till 2018, and has experienced in communication studies, media theories and research. She had worked in some positions during her summer internships. She had worked as a journalism intern in Hürriyet Ankara. She had worked as a reporter and as an editor. She also had worked in EnerjiSA Ankara as a Corporate Communications intern. During her internship, she prepared presentations for the company and prepared media reports. She is interested in reading, research and academic writing.

Damla GÜRKANLI was born in 1995 Ankara, Turkey. She is graduated from Gazi University Private Anatolian High School at Ankara in 2012, her Bachelor of Arts degree in school Communication and Design from

Bilkent University in 2018. During her time at Bilkent University, she worked for Bilkent Radio for a short time and attend relief works. She had worked in some positions during some of the productions. In most of them, he worked as promotional designer. She had completed two summer internships in different positions. She had made editing, photographing and design for magazines during her internships. Ankara where she currently resides. Her personal interests include media, making movies, making design. Damla is an intermediate piano player, and pursuit for the best tasty foods around the globe. When she is not saving animal's lives, Damla can be found playing with her dog or on a nature walk.

Can GÜRMERİÇ was born in Ankara, Turkey in 1994 and has been living in Ankara ever since. Gürmeriç has graduated from TED Ankara College High School in 2012 and studying Communication and Design in Bilkent University ever since. In 2017, Gürmeriç graduated with an education in media studies, video production and advertising. Gürmeriç can speak English fluently, and has basic communication skills for French. Gürmeriç is now getting his Master in Arts in Visual Studies in Bilkent University.
E-mail: cangurmeric@gmail.com

Korcan HEKİMOĞLU was born in Ankara, Turkey in 1995. He went to Gazi College in Ankara for his elementary education. Later, he graduated from Baskent University Private Science High School in 2013. He studied at Bilkent University, Faculty of Communication and Design and graduated in 2018 with an honorary degree. During his study, he took courses specifically focused on advertising, communication, and marketing. He did his internship in a leading advertising agency: Saatchi and Saatchi. During his internship, he worked in strategy department and did many market research and presentations for the challenges of industry leaders such as Turkcell, Vestel, and Yemeksepeti. In 2017, he took strategic marketing in Imperial College Business School for enlarging his existing knowledge in marketing and advertising. Since

December 2016, he is working as a digital marketing responsible for a technology company named Otsimo and managing companies' all digital operations. In upcoming period, he is planning to focus on studies specifically on digital marketing and advertising.

Dr. Dr. Lutz PESCHKE born in 1964, studied Chemistry (Ph.D at University of Heidelberg/Germany) and Media Studies (Ph.D University of Bonn/Germany). Since 1999 head of the Department for Multimedia in iserundschmidt GmbH - Agency for Science Communication. From 2010-2012 lecturer for public relations and science communication in the Department of Media Studies at University Bonn. 2013-2014 lecturer for Media Design in the Faculty of Architecture of Çankaya University in Ankara. Since 2015 lecturer, since 2018 assistant professor for Media and Communication Studies in the Department of Communication and Design at Bilkent University in Ankara. Research interest: science communication, new media studies.

Bora Yağız SİPAHİ was born in 1994 in Rize. He graduated from TED Ankara College in 2012 and continued his academic life at Bilkent University until graduation in 2018 in its Communication and Design Department. During that time, he tried to combine his knowledge with music in his projects. He contributed to two short films as picture and sound editor: Velvet Wander (short music documentary) and Double Six (short thriller). He worked for Excel Communication Management as an intern and GAMA Holding In their corporate communication department. He is also doing music criticism as an amateur pursuit.